Praise for *Prospecting Power*

"After reading *Prospecting Power*, my first thought was, "I wish this book had been available to me when I first started in the business in 1971." After going through my family, friends and relatives, I found it very difficult to cold prospect. This book is simple, direct, and very applicable. The suggestions are great for helping you overcome your fears of prospecting strangers. Not everything will apply to your particular situation, but there is enough general information for you to adapt the principals to fit your personality. *Prospecting Power* would have been a staple of mine to refer to again and again. I recommend it for the beginning IBO and hope it will serve as a reminder for those of us who have been around a long time."

—*Ron Puryear*

"Simply put, Prospecting Power may be the best book you'll ever see on the subject of prospecting. I highly recommend it."

— *Dr. Theron D. Nelsen*

"I have spent 35+ years in the direct sales industry and have taught prospecting to thousands of people. I know how important this skill is in what we do. *Prospecting Power* covers every aspect in the art of meeting people, and it serves as a great outline to help you master your prospecting skills. You will want to read this more than once!"

—*Bill Hawkins*

"Posturing is not taught, it is learned through belief and knowledge. This is a great step-by-step reading on how to build confidence through personal growth and repetition of a defined process. I love it!"

—*Bob Kummer*

"Connecting with people is one of the most important things we need to do to put large organizations together. Throughout this book, Russ takes us step-by-step in doing just that through our thoughts, words, and actions. Take this information and personalize it with your efforts to grow your business."

—*Matt Tsuruda*

"I have known Russ McNeil personally for over 20 years. I have watched him transition and grow as a man, author, and teacher. When I read *Prospecting Power*, it took me back to my early days before the ministry when I was in the insurance industry. I found myself laughing and nodding my head at some of the heartache I went through when learning how to prospect. This would have saved me a lot of hard-learned lessons. *Prospecting Power* will infuse you with confidence as it arms you with time-tested principles of prospecting. Read and enjoy."

—*Paul E. Tsika, pastor/advisor*

"Russ goes through all of the details on what to say, how to say it, and even when to say it. The techniques in *Prospecting Power* will help you take your business to the next level. If you are serious about the business (whatever business it is), you definitely want to have this book. It's not only very practical, but also humorous. You will love seeing how you and your team grow."

—*Nam-Deuk Kim*

"As an IBO, being able to meet new people is an important skill to have. This skill doesn't come naturally to everyone, but it is a skill that anyone can learn. In prospecting, posturing is the key; much like fishing. The fish are out there, you just have to know how to lure them. *Prospecting Power* gives you the map. It also shows you how to bait the hook, how to work the line, and how to reel them in. If you want to fill the boat and win the tournament, this is the one to read."

—*Terry Felber*

"Many people were never taught how to look someone in the eye and make a connection. It comes naturally to some, but many of us didn't inherit that natural talent. *Prospecting Power* gives some great information for business owners on the basics of how to connect with confidence, which is vital in our industry. These are skills that we all can continue to improve upon."

—*Glen Baker*

"When I read *Prospecting Power*, it reminded me of so many of the challenges that new IBOs face. It's always been fairly easy for me to strike up conversations with people because of how God wired me. However, this book will be of great value to those who may be wired differently. A lot depends on your personality and time in the business, but no matter what your personality, *Prospecting Power* serves as a great reminder to everyone that there is 'no impact without contact,' and that contacting people is always our first step in helping others to succeed."

—*Brad Duncan*

"The concepts in *Prospecting Power* can help transform your mindset about talking to strangers. Starting conversations become simple, and friendly discussions with people become fun. Getting comfortable enough to discuss personal ambitions evolves naturally. All of these steps, which initially frighten us, can lead to new friends everywhere we go. The goal is not to change others' ambition, but to identify the ones who are willing to put their ambition into action. Too many new entrepreneurs get overwhelmed by this process and give up on their dreams. This whole experience does not need to be so daunting. It can be enjoyable and rewarding! *Prospecting Power* shows you how."

—*Greg Duncan*

"If you want to set your prospecting ablaze, this book is the match, flame, and kerosene to do it. Your prospecting will be so on FIRE, that you'll be stunned. Russ has done a great job in taking a subject most people avoid and turning it into a step-by-step goldmine. This is a MUST read for anyone that is serious abut their success in prospecting."

—Doug Firebaugh, CEO, PassionFire International, PassionFire.com

"Confidence in prospecting, especially the kind you'll read about in this book, comes from a combination of belief and knowledge. Russ assumes you have the belief. What he expertly teaches in his book, is the knowledge you need to be successful. Follow the principles and specific methods Russ so generously shares and you'll experience great success while helping many others become successful as well. Great job, Russ! Great!"

— Bob Burg, Author, Endless Referrals and co-author
(with John David Mann), The Go-Giver

A growing list of other top producers agree...

"I read this book while traveling to San Antonio to celebrate my wedding anniversary. Despite the significance of the occasion, I lterally could not put the book down. Russ McNeil has put into words what I have been trying to understand and articulate for over 20 years. This book defines prospecting...not just some trite definition, but rather the whole concept. It shows how to execute the entire prospecting process from start to finish and it does all this in a way the reader can apply and duplicate. This book has been missing from MLM for far too long. Thank you, Russ—*Prospecting Rules!* is awesome!"

— T.C.

"If you're new to the industry or even a vetern looking for a fresh approach, this book is jam-packed with simple prospecting techniques and is, by far, the best book on the subject I have ever read. If I were going to write one myself, this would be it. It is, without a doubt, a must read. Go buy 10 copies and give them to your team. It will explode your organization. Don't wait—run to get yours today!"

— S.H.

"Russ McNeil has successfully tackled one of the most challenging aspects of prospecting—the cold market approach—in a simple, logical manner that even the newest networker can benefit from. Although situational prospecting may be considered 'old school' in this age of the internet, as I look across the landscape of our profession, it's clear that 'old school' not only still works, it still works *best*! Our industry needs more books about how to make human contact and create human relationships. *Prospecting Rules!* Is one book fills that void perfectly."

— L.C.

Praise From Down Under

"I missed 100% of the shots I never took."—*Wayne Gretzky*

It goes without saying that Wayne was referring to ice hockey, however, if you're involved in Network-Marketing or Direct-Sales, you realize that he could just as easily have been referring to prospecting. You may never know the costs of not approaching the next person you encounter—perhaps a valuable customer or even a superstar IBO.

Our industry has existed for decades, but prospecting's been around for thousands of years. If you think about it, even Eve prospected Adam to participate in the infamous Apple Scandal. We all prospect every day in one way or another. It's just that sometimes we don't think of it in those terms. For some reason, when we put a product or opportunity behind our prospecting, a road block goes up and suddenly we "forget" how to prospect. In this book, Russ explains the methods that turn the roadblocks into 4-lane highways.

Prospecting Rules! addresses the subject in a way never done before. Russ has dug so deep into prospecting, that if he dug any deeper he would be doing the prospecting for you. From this book, you will learn to turn everyday situations into professional, productive prospecting encounters. In short, applying the information in this book will make your next shot "nothing but net".

Margaret Fuller said, "If you have knowledge, let others light their candles in it." That's exactly what Russ has done. He has revealed the secrets to effective prospecting and it's obvious he didn't hold anything back. The presentation is nothing short of exceptional. It's written in way that makes it easy to understand, easy to laugh, and most importantly, easy to put into action.

Prospecting Rules! is right on the money. Our industry has waited a long time for such a great resource that teaches an easy way to manage prospecting conversations. Now, finally, it's here. I congratulate you for taking the initiative to invest in yourself by improving your prospecting skills. Your biggest reward will come from within.

Troy Rocavert (Australia), co-founder and CEO of Network Marketing Business School, a company specializing in the training and development of individuals and network marketing companies.

PROSPECTING
POWER

Build Your Network with Confidence

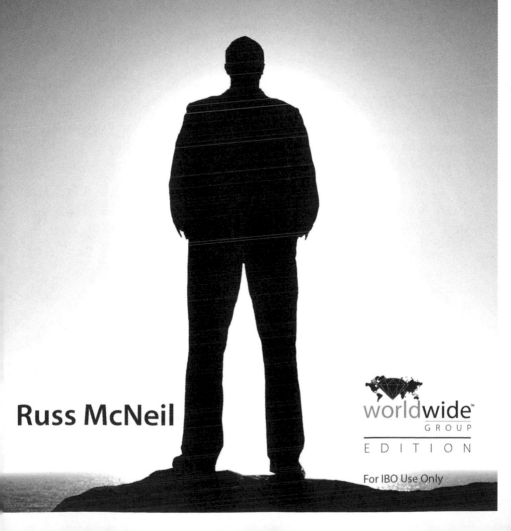

Russ McNeil

world**wide**™
GROUP
E D I T I O N

Prospecting Power

This book and parts thereof may not be reproduced in any form, stored in a retrieval system, or transmitted in any form by any means—electronic, mechanical, photocopy, PowerPoint slides, audio recordings, or other any other format—without prior written permission from the author, except as provided by United States copyright law.

Notice: The information in this book represents techniques, strategies, and concepts that have worked well for the author. Neither the author nor publisher nor reseller make any guarantees regarding the results, or lack thereof, gained by employing the information herein.

This book is a private-label edition of *Prospecting Rules!* branded and retitled for World Wide Group, LLC. To inquire about unbranded versions of this content, visit www.AhaUniversity.com.

Hey! Read this!

If you find this content helpful, you may also enjoy Russ's complimentary newsletter which is jam-packed with other great prospecting stuff. Subscriptions are available at AhaUniversity.com.

ISBN: 978-0-9899582-5-7

Printed in United States of America

Contents

Acknowledgements

God is willing to share His talents, but not His glory. In the case of this book, it's obvious that He shared His talents, because it wouldn't have been possible any other way. I enthusiastically give Him all the glory for it.

I am also compelled to express my deepest gratitude to several mentors who have sown time, knowledge, and wisdom into my life:

> **David Hott**—You are the one who first introduced me to this amazing business. With one phone call, you set in motion, a chain of events having an eternal impact on people you have never met. It has been a fantastic journey and will thrill me as long as I live.

> **Larry Lenamond**—You whetted my appetite for personal development by demonstrating its fruit in your own life. I am a better human being because of it. (The people who knew me prior to personal development are even more thankful).

> **Dean Lindsay**—It was you who first showed me that it's God behind this project, not Russ. You've been there from day one—mentoring and encouraging me as I travel the journey of professional speaking and authorship. You excel at both speaking and writing, and in true pay-it-forward fashion, you continue to sow your knowledge and experience into me. There's no telling how many mistakes I've avoided simply because you took the time to share. Your success is clearly visible as a golden thread woven into the tapestry of my own.

Special recognition is in order for Sandy Himel. Your rare mix of creativity and meticulous attention to detail proved invaluable in the layout of this book. Furthermore, your insightful input polished the basic design to a gleaming luster. Only someone sharing my tilted sense of humor could have filled the role to so superbly. Sandy, this book is part you.

Thanks to Ron Puryear and Paul Tsika for generosity that defies words, to Brian Mast (Pilot Communications Group) for continuous streams of insight regarding production and marketing, and to three extraordinary individuals: Daniel Ferguson, Denna Ferguson, and Aaron Alaniz for spiritual support; the world may never know how much you've meant to this project, but I do and so does the One Whom we serve.

Lastly, I need to express appreciation for my one-in-a-million wife, Tammy. Your patience and discernment are God's gift to you. You are God's gift to me. It is for you that I build our businesses.

Foreword

by John David Mann

"Go ahead, make my day."
"Houston, we have a problem."
"I'll have what she's having."
"Work around here?"
"Attica! Attica!"
"Rosebud…"

How can a tiny handful of words speak such volumes? None of these lines is longer than five words, but each evokes an amazing range of ideas, experiences, emotions and attitudes. It's the screenwriter's Haiku magic, that ability to capture the depth and breadth of human experience in a little scatter of simple words.

The very same thing that happens in these classic film scenes also happens in your prospecting conversations. Events and sometimes even destinies turn on the simplest lines of dialog in that casual encounter called "opening conversation with a stranger."

Russ McNeil takes a master screenwriter/director's eye to this single scene and devotes 155 brilliant pages to deconstructing it in careful, thorough detail. By the time you've finished reading these pages, you will understand exactly how this scene works and be well on your way to recreating it yourself, spinning your own miniature masterpieces in variation after variation. This is a bold claim, but I make it with confidence because Russ knows his stuff, and PROSPECTING POWER! is the real thing. If you're looking for gold, you've got it in your hands.

Often when reading books about sales, prospecting or networking, I start to feel claustrophobic, as if walls of information are closing in and I urgently have to memorize it all, because my future encounters with people who might be viable prospects will be a test I can hope to pass only based on how well I have crammed.

This is not a happy feeling.

I'm happy to report that reading Russ's book is nothing like that. Quite the opposite, in fact: I enjoy ambling through its pages as much as I would strolling through a great novel. There's plenty of information in here, all right; every page is thick with thought-provoking insights. But it doesn't feel *complicated*. As I turn the pages, instead of muttering, "Okay, I'm gonna have to remember this," I find myself saying, "Right! Of course!" It feels less like formulas to be memorized, and more like descriptions of some cool dance moves I can't wait to try out.

By the way, of the six quotes above ("Go ahead, make my day," etc.), five are from the American Film Institute's *100 Top Movie Quotes*. I'll leave it you to guess which one is from the book you're about to read. (Hint: it's not "I'll have what she's having," though using that as a conversation-starter is an interesting thought.) You'll learn all about it in *Curiosity Paid the Cat,* starting on page 64.

We like to say of our industry, *"Anyone* can do this business." We like to think of this as the ultimate equal-opportunity opportunity, the epitome of democracy in free enterprise. But there is no getting around this central fact of the industry: *to be really successful at it, you have to get really good at it*. We like to think that all you have to do is be yourself, be sincere, be a product of the product: "Share your enthusiasm, let the tools tell the story — and the rest will take care of itself." But that's not how it is.

Our business is a *profession*. A profession of amateurs, granted (*amateurs* in the best sense: one who does what she does for the love of it) — but a profession nonetheless, and the central skill of this profession is <u>knowing how to conduct a friendly, genuine, effective prospecting conversation</u>. There are those rare few individuals who possess this skill innately, for whom this conversation comes naturally. For the rest of us, Russ has finally taken the Swiss watch apart, shown exactly how it works, and put it back together again.

I'll have what Russ is having.

John David Mann is co-author (with Bob Burg) of the national bestseller *The Go-Giver* and author of *The Zen of MLM*. He was cofounder and senior editor of *Upline* and editor in chief of *Network Marketing Lifestyles* and *Networking Times*. He edited and produced John Milton Fogg's *The Greatest Networker in the World* (1992), which became the industry's defining book of the decade and sold more than one million copies in eight languages. He also worked with John Assaraf and Murray Smith writing *The Answer* (2008), with Paul Zane Pilzer writing *The Next Millionaires* (2005) and with Jeff Olson writing *The Slight Edge* (2004). John has also been an active direct selling leader for more than twenty years; during the 1990's he built an organization of over 100,000 distributors that earned a personal income of several million dollars.

Dear Reader,

This book is not about me. It's about you. Even so, I am compelled to sprinkle some of my own story throughout. There is only one reason for doing so — to give you hope. If *I* can learn to do what is in this book, then *you* can too.

It's a well-known saying: "The mass of men lead lives of quiet desperation." Henry David Thoreau penned these famous words over a century ago. I believe they are truer today than when he first wrote them. Fortunately, they don't apply to you. As an active IBO, you have hope. You have to goals to pursue. You have an alternative to the desperation. All you have to do is go out and share it.

The key to success in sales is: to have a good story to tell, to tell it well, and to tell it often. By being in the industry, you already have a good story to tell. It is my hope that the information presented on these pages will empower you to tell it well, to tell it often, and to have some fun while you're doing it.

When executed properly, our unique business model represents a huge blessing to everyone involved. It is my prayer that this book will empower you to pass on the blessings that your business represents. Because when that happens, we all benefit—the prospect, you, and to a certain degree, me. That's a perfect example of mutual-win, which after all, is *precisely* what this book is about.

Now, go knock 'em *alive!*

Russ

Every human being has a work to carry on within, duties to perform abroad, influence to exert, which are peculiarly his, and which no conscious but his own can teach.

— *William Ellery Channing*

chapter One

Getting Started

When your warm market gives you the cold shoulder,
start a warm conversation with a cool stranger.
—*Russ McNeil*

Who Should Read This Book

If you are new to the industry, the concepts in this book will prove especially beneficial. Promoting a business opportunity to people you don't know is a unique type of activity. It's easy to get discouraged before your efforts begin to pay off. By applying what you read here, you can accelerate the learning process and get tangible results sooner.

If you're an experienced IBO, you will already be familiar with many of the concepts herein. Even so, you are bound to find some fresh ideas. At the very least, the principles described will help you define a structure for your own prospecting style.

No Theory Here

This book is not about theory. It is about practical concepts that get results. While it does go into some of the psychology behind the principles, it goes beyond

> In **theory,** there is no difference between theory and practice. In **practice,** there is no relationship between them.
>
> —Unknown

that. It also contains actual words and phrases that, with practice, will generate tangible results. The suggestions work because they are based on sound principles — not on one person's ability to exert his unique brand of influence.

Do Your Own Thing

This book includes mock dialogues to illustrate the concepts in this book. Each mock dialogue represents an excerpt of the overall conversation that includes some of the very words and phrases I use when I'm out in the world prospecting. Don't get the impression that these are

> It's all right to be a copycat. Just make sure that you copy the right cat.
>
> —D. Self

the only words and phrases that will work. Such a notion is simply not true. Eventually, you will want to develop your own prospecting style, which will include words and phrases that fit your personality. Any prospecting style will work as long as it's based on the correct principles.

How to Use This Book

You may apply any of the principles independently of the others. They are however, much more effective when you apply them in combination with one another.

One chapter is dedicated to each principle—not only to describe the principle but also to give examples of how to incorporate it into your prospecting conversations. At first, it may not be readily apparent how to combine a particular principle with the others. That's because, initially, the explanation will be out of context. Don't let this seem confusing. A later chapter ties all the principles together.

To get the most out of this book, read it twice. The first time, read it cover-to-cover to get a feel for the philosophies and attitudes it represents. The second time, concentrate on the core chapters covering the principles themselves. As you reread the chapters, you will have prior insight on all of the principles and it will be more obvious how they complement each other.

Easy Does It

I didn't simply wake up one day and suddenly have a complete understanding of the eight principles you are about to learn. It took years for me to "discover" many of the ideas in this book. I use the word discover not because I originated the concepts, but because I had to uncover them on my own. I didn't have the benefit of taking notes while someone else explained the in's and out's of prospecting strangers.

If you study and apply the principles described in this book, it won't take years for you to become an expert at prospecting. Even so, the development of your prospecting skills won't be instantaneous. It will take some time. Don't rush. As you begin to see results with one principle, add another until gradually you have incorporated them all.

An Order to the Madness

Within the book, the principles are presented in a chronological order based on where they typically fall in the conversation. Read them in this order.

However, I recommend a different order as you begin to employ them. The first principle to implement is *Mental Judo* (Chapter 10). The second one is *Casualize & Minimize* (Chapter 13). After you figure out these two, add the others in any order you'd like.

Terminology

There are several key terms used throughout the book. They are:

Rep—short for representative. It is a generic term used to mean someone actively involved in a Direct-Sales or Network-Marketing opportunity. Common industry titles include associate, broker, distributor, independent business owner (IBO), and representative. This book uses IBO because that's what you are, it's easy to read, and most importantly, because it's easy for me to type.

Tools—most companies encourage the use of professionally produced marketing collateral to promote their opportunities. Such collateral may come in the form of tapes, magazines, CD-ROM's, or DVD's. This book uses the terms tools and prospecting tools interchangeably to refer to all these items.

Jack—you will see this name sprinkled throughout the book. Jack is the name of a fictitious prospect. We pick on him incessantly and without mercy. Sorry, Jack. (No wonder he's not so crazy about the industry.) Poor Jack—maybe one day he'll wise up.

Team building, team-based opportunity, and the industry—these terms, and others like them, are used throughout as synonyms for Network-Marketing and Direct Sales and Party Plans. Philosophically, these business models are quite different. However, from the standpoint of prospecting, they are too similar to draw a distinction. In this book, the synonyms are used as generic references to include these business models. Read them in the context that makes sense for you.

What's the Big Deal about Strangers?

When first introduced to the industry, I was like most other people when they get started. I was excited. I knew that all my friends and relatives would see the same potential that I did, especially with all the credibility I had with them. I was certain that the big bucks would be flowing freely in no time.

Imagine my surprise.

For starters, none of my friends or relatives had even the slightest interest in my opportunity. I quickly discovered that any credibility I had with them did not extend into the realm of business opportunities. The people who knew me simply did not see me as a font of business acumen.

Imagine that.

I ran into another obstacle as well. It was only much later that I realized the nature of the obstacle: the more a person knew about me, the more they knew about my past failures. What reason did they have to assume that my new business venture into would be any different?

> *A prophet is not without honor but in his own country, and among his own kin, and in his own house.*
>
> —Mark 6:4, *KJV*

So there I was. I had a fabulous opportunity that I was excited about and believed in, but no one I knew seemed to care. I found myself wondering what to do next. Then it occurred to me that I live in a city with five million other people. It also occurred to me that I only needed a few of them to attain financial independence. All I had to do was find this precious few and have them join my team. So goes the first law of prospecting:

1st law of prospecting

The list of people who *don't* know you is infinitely larger than the list of people who *do* know you.

Once you form the habit of prospecting strangers, you will never run out of prospects. Think about it — people are turning 18 faster than you can get to them. How could you ever run out of people to approach? This law gives you a major advantage in building your business. Since you believe in your product and opportunity, you should want to share it with the people you already know and care for. Many reps, however, will get better results talking to strangers. Ironically, you have more credibility with strangers than with your friends and family. The second law of prospecting spells this out:

2nd law of prospecting

People who *don't* know you will take you more seriously than the ones who *do* know you.

Prospects form opinions based on what they know and what they see. Jack (or whatever your prospect's name is), will evaluate you on what he knows about your personal track record and how well you relate to him. When you first meet Jack, he has no knowledge of your past successes or failures. His opinion of you (and of your offer) isn't influenced by your resume. All he has to go on is his first impression.

That's good news! There is an unlimited supply of people willing to take you seriously if you relate well to them. In fact, you could really mess it up with a bunch of them and still build a successful business. Now that you have that monkey off your back, take a deep breath and relax. Besides, if you don't start meeting new people, what will you do when you get to the end of the list of people you already know? That's the challenge…and the reason for this book.

Building a Team with Strangers

Since I got such a chilly reception from my so-called *warm* market, I set out to build a team with people I did not yet know. First, there were questions that demanded answers:

- Where would I find the people with which to build a team?
- How would I go about meeting them?
- What would I say to them when I did meet them?

Instinctively, I knew the answer to the first question. We pass people every day who are prime candidates for our opportunities. Unfortunately, that is exactly what most reps do — pass them. Think about your daily routine and the places you frequent — grocery stores, restaurants, elevators, and my personal favorite, gas stations. Have you ever turned the tables on a telemarketer? See, you passed another one. The third law of prospecting summarizes this idea:

> # 3rd law of prospecting
>
> Some of the people we pass in everyday life would be hugely successful in our business, but unless we prospect them, we'll never know which ones they are.

The other questions caused me real concern. How would I approach them and what would I say? I quickly discovered that no one seemed to have complete answers to these questions. Obviously, there were people who had methods and styles of approaches that were working for them. The challenge was that no one seemed to be teaching the in's and out's of prospecting strangers. Oh sure, there was plenty of teaching about specific one-liners, but what was missing was an organized strategy of conversation that prepared the prospect for responding to the one-liners. The purpose of this book is to fill that void.

Prospecting vs. Sponsoring

Prospecting is a vital aspect of team building. Keep in mind, though, that it is only a part of the process. For the purpose of this book, we draw a distinction between prospecting and sponsoring.

Prospecting is the process of approaching someone you do not know and using conversation to determine if he or she has an interest in exploring your opportunity. Sponsoring is the process of sharing the details of your opportunity with the intent of enrolling them as a IBO on your team.

This book focuses on the development of prospecting skills. Sponsoring is an entirely differently subject. The sponsoring process is more specific to your particular opportunity and this book will not discuss it. As far as this book is concerned, the goal of the prospecting process is to get a tool into the hands of an interested prospect and following up a day or two later.

Magic Questions

Author's Note: This section briefly introduces the term "magic question". The concept of magic questions is important enough to warrant a separate discussion so a later chapter covers the topic in detail.

What in the world is a magic question? A magic question is the capstone of a prospecting conversation. Magic questions determine whether the prospect wants to learn about your opportunity. An effective one makes it easy for the Jack to say yes and hard for him to say no. The entire prospecting process guides the conversation to the magic question.

The Prospecting Moment

A prospecting moment is the point in a conversation that represents the optimum time for you to ask your magic question. The goal of the prospecting conversation is to create a fertile verbal environment in which the prospecting moment can occur naturally and within the available time.

Once you have mastered the principles of prospecting, you will orchestrate prospecting conversations at will. You will be able to gauge the timing of the conversation and know just when to initiate the prospecting moment. The entire process will transpire so naturally that the prospect will never realize what's happened. You will be an artist and every conversation will be your canvas. If a geek-speaking software engineer can learn to meet and prospect total strangers in face-to-face conversations, then you certainly can.

chapter Two

The Magic of Conditioning

The difference between try and triumph is a little *umph*.
—*Marvin Phillips*

Quarterbacks and Prospectors

Consider the following three people and their occupations: a doctor, a commercial truck driver, and a pro football quarterback. What do they have in common? You guessed it — conditioning. They made deliberate preparations for their chosen careers. Each of them invested time and money in the education essential to their respective professions.

When you see a man at the top of a mountain, you know that he didn't fall there.

—Coleman Orr

After acquiring the initial book knowledge, these professionals learned to apply the knowledge. Only through consistent practice can you complete the learning process.

Developing strong prospecting skills requires investment of a different sort. The largest investment you will make to master prospecting is the time you spend on personal development. Three strategies in particular will condition you for taking full advantage of the principles in this book:

- Use affirmations
- Sharpen your people skills
- Practice what you learn

Experience is not the best teacher. Someone else's experience is.

Strategy #1: Use Affirmations

Affirmations, a form of self-talk, are the single most powerful tool you have to condition yourself for prospecting. Self-talk is what you say when you talk to and about yourself. It includes the things you say aloud as well as the things you say internally. Self-talk dictates a person's behavior by molding his innermost beliefs. Positive self-talk will produce desirable results and negative self-talk will produce undesirable results. Affirmations are things you say that induce positive self-talk.

The concept of self-talk is abstract. So much so, that for two years after I first heard about it, I completely disregarded it. The concept seemed foreign and illogical, and I refused to try it. Looking back, I realize that those two years have cost me many thousands of dollars. I encourage you to learn from my mistake. Embrace self-talk; the results are dramatic.

Self-talk is the subject of countless books. Building a case for and explaining the entire mechanism of self-talk is beyond the scope of *PROSPECTING POWER!* Even so, it is a powerful tool and it warrants a short explanation.

How Self-talk Works

What follows, is a brief, no-frills overview of self-talk:

- The subconscious mind will focus on the most dominant message.
- The subconscious mind receives input from hearing.
- The subconscious mind does not distinguish between fact and fiction.
- The subconscious mind is the gateway to our beliefs.
- Our beliefs determine our actions.
- Our actions determine our results.

> *One advantage of talking to yourself is that you know at least somebody's listening.*
> —Franklin P. Jones

When we hear the same message repeatedly, it becomes the dominant message. Since the subconscious mind cannot tell the difference between fact and fiction, over time, the dominant message develops into a belief. The belief, in turn, will irresistibly dictate our actions.

Applying Affirmations to Prospecting

When we first get involved in team-building, most of us have at least some beliefs that inhibit our prospecting efforts. This is a nice way of saying that most of us have some hang-ups. If you do have hang-ups, you will need to deal with them *before* you can take full advantage of the principles in this book. Some of the more common hang-ups include:

- A belief that for your opportunity to work, you must take advantage of or manipulate others;
- A belief that others will perceive you as taking advantage of them;
- A belief that when someone tells you "no," it diminishes your own ability to succeed;

These beliefs are false, yet they can paralyze you to the point that you never offer your opportunity beyond a handful of people. By applying affirmations, you can override these unproductive beliefs with productive ones.

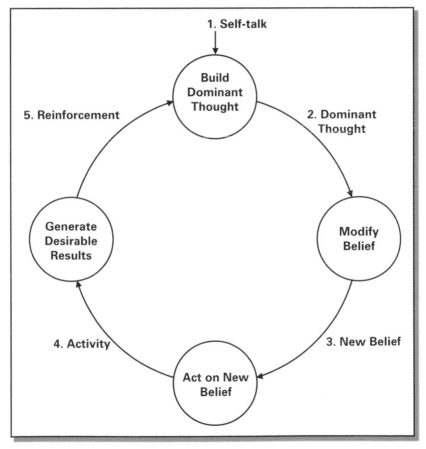

Figure 1: The Self-talk Cycle

Note: The author's complimentary newsletter, Prospecting with Purpose, includes specific prospecting affirmations. Visit ProspectingRules.com to subscribe."

Strategy #2: Sharpen Your People Skills

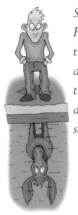

Samson slew 600 Philistines with the jawbone of an ass, and every day thousands of sales are killed with the same weapon.

—Jack Nadel

Your ability to relate to different people has a direct bearing on the success of your prospecting efforts. When it comes to approaching strangers, quick connections are invaluable. By developing your people skills, you will be able to relate quickly to a wide range of prospects. The more refined your people skills, the more rapidly you will be able to make the connections.

People skills are not innate, Rest assured that when you meet someone who is good with people, his or her skills were cultivated intentionally. The less value you see in developing people skills, the more you need to do just that. Personal development is crucial to all aspects of team building, especially prospecting. Reps with underdeveloped people skills often drive prospects away in the first encounter. That's too early in the process for the rep's coach (aka upline) to step in and save the day.

Learn to become a better you. The best way to learn about improving your people skills is through books and audio programs. This list below identifies some of the resources that I use even today to keep my own prospecting skills sharp.

Title	Author
How to Win Friends & Influence People	Dale Carnegie
The Go-Giver	Bob Burg & John David Mann
The Greatest Salesman in the World	Og Mandino
Hung by the Tongue	Francis P. Martin

Strategy #3: Practice, Practice, Practice

Practice makes perfect. When it comes to prospecting, perfection is optional — practice is not.

From Ignorance To Mastery

We all know that the more you do something, the better you get at it. Scientists have developed a model that describes the process of progressing from ignorance to mastery. It's called the Conscious Competence Learning Matrix. This matrix is composed of four phases. By definition you must traverse these in sequence. Let's look at how this model applies to prospecting strangers.

1. Unconscious Incompetence

This phase describes someone who is unaware of what they don't know. Before you became an IBO, you were in this phase. Until you started your business, there was no reason for you to consider the subject of prospecting strangers. Thus, you had no reason to know about prospecting. You didn't know what you didn't know about prospecting. Clearly, you aren't in this phase now. If you were, you would not be reading this book.

2. Conscious Incompetence

This phase describes people who are consciously aware of the fact that they lack some key skill. In other words, they realize that they don't know what they need to know. If you are new to the process of approaching strangers with a business opportunity, you are in this phase.

If at first you don't succeed, then skydiving is not for you.

— Henny Youngman

When you first begin to employ the information in *PROSPECTING POWER!*, you may have a tendency to become discouraged. Keep in mind that you aren't skydiving. With prospecting, you can get it all wrong and still live to try again. It will take both practice and time, to move from incompetence to competence. You're not in competition with anyone but yourself so give yourself permission to take the time. The results are worth every minute.

3. Conscious Competence

A person in this phase performs the skill competently, but it takes concentration and deliberate effort to do so. If you continue to practice the principles of prospecting, you will eventually find yourself in this phase. In the conscious competence phase, you are fully aware of how, when, and where to apply the principles, but it requires conscious focus. In this phase, you will see tangible results on a regular basis. The more often you practice the principles, the quicker you will become consciously competent.

Warning: Once you have entered this phase, you may actually have fun prospecting.

4. Unconscious Competence

> *The hard must become habit. The habit must become easy. The easy must become beautiful.*
> —Doug Henning, magician

A person in this phase has mastered the skill to the point that the skill has become second nature. The person performs the skill on automatic pilot with little or no conscious effort. Have you ever driven from your workplace to home and when you arrived, you realize that you don't even remember making the trip? That's unconscious competence. You perform without having to think about it. If you employ the principles consistently, at some point you will transition into this final phase. Once this happens, the skill of prospecting will be second nature.

Practice Will Overcome the Fear

For many people, building a business like ours can be intimidating. It requires you to develop new skills and to apply these skills in strange and foreign ways. Indeed, for many reps, the most intimidating aspect of team building is the prospecting process.

When I first started prospecting for team members, I had no prior related experience. My formal education was highly technical. I had never received training to prepare me for dealing with people. Merely talking to strangers was uncomfortable. The notion of approaching them with a business opportunity nearly paralyzed me with fear.

As an inexperienced IBO, I was using undeveloped skills to approach total strangers about something I knew virtually nothing about. No wonder I was afraid. I knew just enough to be dangerous and danger is *not* my idea of fun.

Understanding the Fear

Thankfully, I had the blessing of a mentor who helped me to understand fear and how to overcome it. This life-changing teaching included three powerful truths:

1. Fear Comes From Lack of Knowledge.

We fear the dark because we don't know what it is hiding. We fear falling because we don't know how bad the sudden stop will hurt. We fear

> *Fear always springs from ignorance.*
> —Ralph Waldo Emerson

prospecting because we don't feel prepared for the prospect's questions. If we have the knowledge to respond to his questions, we know what to say. If we know what to say, there is no fear.

2. Knowledge Comes From Experience.

The more you do, the more you learn. As you gain experience in prospecting, you will come to the earth-shattering revelation that all prospects share the same list of

> *A man carrying a cat by the tail learns something he can learn no other way.*
> —Mark Twain

responses. The fact is, that the list of prospect objections is actually quite short. With experience, you will learn how to deal with the most common responses. You will know enough to prospect effectively.

3. Experience comes from practice.

You should find this statement liberating. This single truth empowers you to overcome the fear of prospecting. Practice allows you to apply theory to the real world. Through practice, you will get the experience to gain the knowledge that, in turn, will eradicate the fear. The more you practice, the less you will fear.

Following this line of reasoning, the logical conclusion is that if you practice enough the fear will evaporate. That is exactly what happened to me and, if you practice diligently, that is exactly what will happen to you. The good news is that it will happen. The bad news is that it will not happen instantly because it is a process. Here's more good news — the process is completely predictable.

Stretching the Comfort Bubble

> *Do the thing and you will have the power.*
> — Ralph Waldo Emerson

I call the process of practicing through the fear stretching the comfort bubble.

Think of your comfort zone as a bubble. Everything within the bubble is comfortable. Things inside the bubble are familiar. You have complete knowledge of everything inside the bubble. There are no strangers in the bubble. The bubble is safe, a place of refuge. Unfortunately, the prospect exists outside the bubble. A conversation with a prospect is likely to be uncomfortable. If you are like I used to be, it is *extremely* uncomfortable. The idea is to stretch your comfort bubble to the point that it is large enough to include the prospect.

How do you stretch your comfort bubble? Believe it not, your comfort bubble is surprisingly easy to stretch. Just follow these three easy steps: prospect, prospect, and then prospect some more. As long as you keep these in the right order, your bubble will stretch. When you use every opportunity to practice prospecting, you are applying a constant pressure on the walls of your bubble. You will notice the stretching is taking place when you realize that you're not as apprehensive about starting conversations with strangers. With a little more stretching, you'll become comfortable guiding the conversation. After some more stretching, you will become comfortable creating the prospecting moment.

Who's the Oddball Now?

Years ago, I listened to an audio tape about one particular aspect of prospecting. At some point on the tape, the speaker said, "If you practice this call enough, you will eventually get so good at it, that when the prospect says no, you'll think he's odd." I was a prospecting novice when I first listened to that tape. I remember thinking, "Yeah, right…whatever." I just could not visualize anyone being that good, let alone me.

One day, a year or so later, I called a prospect and as usual, I used the script I had memorized from the tape. The prospect was flattered that I had called, but wasn't at all inclined to look at other opportunities. He graciously declined and I thanked him for his time. As soon as I hung up the phone, I said, "What an oddball." The trainer on the tape was right! I literally used the word oddball!

When you first start prospecting, you may feel a little odd about it. Once you attain unconscious competence, your perspective will make a 180° turn. As a prospector in the final phase, you will be so competent, that when a prospect declines your invitation, you may think that *he's* the oddball.

chapter Three

Making Contact

I am prepared to meet anyone, but whether anyone is prepared
for the great ordeal of meeting me, is another matter.

—*Mark Twain*

Applying the principles of prospecting requires conversation. Naturally, for the conversation to occur, someone has to speak first. Since you're the one with something to share, you go first.

For a few reps, starting conversation with strangers will be easy, maybe even fun. For many, it will be slightly morecomfortablethanskinny-dipping in quicksand. Realize that while most people are not comfortable initiating

> We cannot possibly let ourselves get frozen into regarding everyone we do not know as an absolute stranger.
>
> — Albert Schweitzer

conversation, they do enjoy participating in it. In other words, prospects will be glad to talk to you if you speak first. When I first heard that statement, I didn't believe it. Of course, at that point, I was inexperienced and basking in the luxury of ignorance. Once I began to get some experience of my own, I found out that in general, people really do enjoy conversation. In fact, it is safe to say that most people are starving for it.

Make a Positive First Impression

Before you initiate contact, prepare yourself. Your demeanor will set the tone of the entire encounter. The unspoken signals you give off can shout so loudly that the prospect may never hear your words. If you want to attract others, then be attractive. The next few sections may seem like common sense. Unfortunately, sometimes common sense is not so common.

Be constantly aware of your facial expressions. This statement has nothing whatsoever to do with the appearance of your facial features. It's referring to how you are "wearing" your attitude on your face. It is hard to attract others when you have a scowl on your face. Don't overdo it. It's not necessary to go through your day grinning like a wall-mounted possum. You should however, attempt to sustain a pleasant expression. If you frown all the way up to the moment you and the prospect make eye contact, it's too late to smile. A sudden change of expression at that point is not genuine and the prospect will see you as a phony — and rightly so.

Another part of your demeanor is how you carry yourself. If you drag your feet when you walk, you appear lazy. Stand erect. Slumping over makes you appear defeated. Walk with purpose. People follow people who have a sense of who they are. If you want to have a team to lead, then carry yourself like a leader *before* you have the team.

Looking upbeat and moving confidently are both important, but they are a waste of time if your speech is contradicting them. From the standpoint of speech, one of the worst things you can do is mumble. Mumbling shows a lack of confidence, so speak clearly.

Another common speech mistake is talking too fast. When you first begin to prospect strangers, you may be nervous. This is perfectly normal. Don't let the fact that you're nervous make you even more nervous. If you are like I used to be, nervousness makes you talk fast. (That's because your fear has the adrenaline flowing). If you come across as nervous, it may cause the prospect to keep his guard up. If nothing else, talking fast will make you hard to understand. Keep practicing. The nervousness will subside over time. Give yourself time to grow with the process. The worst thing you can do is let your apprehension keep you from prospecting at all.

Classify the Target

As you prospect strangers, you will encounter two types of prospects: stationary targets and fixed targets. In referring to the prospects as "targets," we are merely having some fun with our subject. Proper prospecting is always a win-win proposition.

A stationary target is a prospect that you know you can have access to on a regular basis. Typically, you will consider a target stationary because of his location or job. For example, the person running a dry cleaner that you frequent is a stationary target. You know from experience that the store's manager always seems to be there when you drop in. You have an advantage when prospecting stationary targets because you have plenty of opportunities to build rapport with them over an extended period.

A moving target is a prospect that you meet in passing. The term moving does not mean that you follow him around like a puppy looking for a chance to start a conversation. By moving, I mean, that in all likelihood, you and the prospect will cross paths only once—right now. You only get one chance to prospect a moving target. An example of a moving target is the person on the opposite side of a gas pump you are using.

Eye Contact

In some scenarios, especially with moving targets, the moment of eye contact is the best time to initiate a conversation. It isn't imperative that you wait for eye contact, but when eye contact does occur, it is the most natural time to start. If you look at each other and no one speaks, you may find it awkward to strike up a conversation later.

Opening Lines

An opening line is a question or statement designed to initiate conversation. Don't confuse opening lines with magic questions. The purpose of an opening line is merely to get a conversation started. Depending on how the conversation unfolds, you may or may not ever get to the magic question. Because of the need to

> *Don't knock the weather; nine-tenths of the people couldn't start a conversation if it didn't change once in a while.*
>
> —Kin Hubbard

engage quickly, effective opening lines are essential with moving targets. In contrast, opening lines are not as crucial with stationary targets because with stationary targets, it's easy to develop rapport over time.

Examples

I have several opening lines that work well. This section lists some of them along with sample scenarios in which they are applied. Most of the conversations I have with moving targets start with one of these lines. That's because even though I don't prospect everyone I meet, I use the same opening lines with *all* new acquaintances. As you study them, keep in mind, that over time, you'll develop your own lines that fit your own personality and prospecting style.

Scenario 1

You are pumping gas. There is a person on the other side of the pump filling his car as well. You decide to initiate contact.

Y:	How's it goin'?
P:	Pretty good.
Y:	Merely pretty good? I'm sorry. (straight face)
P:	Actually, it's going great.
Y:	Ah, so you lied to me the first time. (grin)

I provide this as the first example because it is the approach I use the most often (same words, different scenarios). Many of the conversations follow this script word for word. If Jack does chuckle, you're off to a great start. Even if he doesn't express amusement, you still have a conversation started.

Scenario 2

You are in a casual restaurant. At the table next to you, is a person reading a newspaper. After watching for a short while, you observe that the person is completely engrossed in the newspaper.

Y:	Is there any good news in there?
P:	Not really.
Y:	I gave up on the news a long time ago.

Think of this line as a test probe. Sometimes, lone readers are alone by choice. Sometimes they have no interest in a conversation. After this probe, you will have a good idea if the prospect will participate in further conversation.

Scenario 3

You're in a casual restaurant. At the table next to you, is a person working on a laptop. You notice that he also has papers strewn about. Perhaps his phone is lying out on the table.

Y:	You in sales?
P:	Yeah.
Y:	Really? What do you sell?

You may think that assuming he's in sales is risky. It isn't. Experience shows that he probably is in sales. Even if he's not, you still got the conversation started. In that case, instead of asking what he sells, ask him what it is that he does do. The point is not whether you guess correctly. The point is to start a conversation.

Scenario 4

You're on the fifth floor of the office building where you work. It's lunch time and you press the down elevator button in anticipation of leaving the building. As you enter the elevator, you see that another person is already aboard. You reach out to press the ① button, but stop short upon seeing that it's already lit. Now, put an expression of surprise on your face, look at the other person, and say this: "How did you know I was going to the first floor?"

It will be hard for the prospect to resist the urge to chuckle in this scenario. Congratulations, you're on your way.

Notice that these first scenarios begin with a question. When you ask a question, common rules of conversation compel the prospect to respond. Questions are a powerful and natural way to initiate conversation.

Scenario 5

You run into a well-groomed man in a coffee shop mid-morning on a weekday. He is dressed casually, but sharp, maybe even in nice short pants. He is sitting relaxed and not engaged in work of any type. Perhaps he is reading the *Wall Street Journal*. You have the impression that he's an executive enjoying a day off.

Y:	I need your job!
P:	Why's that?
Y:	Are you kidding? Relaxed and casual on a weekday. What's your secret?

In my experience, this is one of the easiest conversations to pursue. Why? Because the more successful Jack is, the more confident he is and in general, the more open-minded he will be. After the above discourse, you will know whether to proceed. One time I used this exact approach and the prospect turned out to be the founder of an international Network-Marketing company! Naturally, he wasn't a candidate for my opportunity, but the resulting conversation proves that the principles of prospecting really do get results.

Take these lines and use them as is or create your own. The main concept here is to have a small set of opening lines that you draw upon for use with prospect after prospect.

When the Prospect Speaks First

> It is generally agreed that "hello" is an appropriate greeting because, if you entered a room and said "goodbye," it could confuse a lot of people.
>
> —Dolph Sharp

Occasionally, the prospect will beat you to the punch and speak to you before you speak to him. These people are asking to be prospected. If you don't want to disappoint them, have some responses ready. Typically, they will ask something like "How's it goin'?" Here are some of my favorite responses:

- If I was any better, I'd have to charge admission just to say "hi."
- I'll tell you what: if I was doin' any better, I'd have to sit on both hands to keep from hugging myself!
- If I was any better, I'd be twins. And trust me—that's a scary thought.
- Well, I'm able to sit up and take nourishment.
- Who wants to know?
- Just wonderful, but I'm getting better. How 'bout you?
- If I was any better, you wouldn't be able to stand it. The question is how are you doing?
- Well, I was doing excellent, but now I'm doing even better.
- Well, when I woke up, I didn't see red velvet or candles. I suppose that's a good start.

While none of these responses is outrageously hilarious, they typically will cause the prospect to at least chuckle. The key is to have a response that makes the prospect think, "That was different. I like this person."

Now What?

As you read the example dialogues in this chapter, they may seem open-ended and incomplete. You may be wondering what to do next, what to say next, where to go from here. Be patient. You are just getting started. The principles explain everything. At the end of the book, you will find an entire example dialogue that ties it all together.

chapter **Four**

Magic Questions

Any sufficiently advanced technology is indistinguishable
from magic.

—*Arthur C. Clarke*

As mentioned in the introduction, a magic question is the capstone of the prospecting conversation. In fact, most of the conversation is dedicated to setting the stage for the magic question.

What is a Magic Question?

A magic question uncovers whether the prospect wants to learn about your business opportunity. *Read the previous sentence again.* There is a huge difference between learning about and joining. Always keep this distinction in mind.

What is so magical about a magic question? Think about it. You ask a total stranger if he would like to learn about some nebulous opportunity that you don't explain and the prospect says "yes". If that isn't magic, what is?

What a Magic Question is *Not*

It is paramount that you understand what a magic question is not.

Not An Explanation

A magic question is not the point in your conversation to explain your opportunity. In fact, in the initial conversation with a prospect, resist every temptation to explain your opportunity. You are the messenger, not the message. Let your prospecting tools be the message.

Your company's prospecting tools incorporate multiple aspects (i.e., visual, emotional) to intrigue the prospect. Chances are you do not know how to deliver a message with the same impact as the tools. Even if you do have the skills, ask yourself this: Does your team have the skills? If you have the skills, and your team doesn't, then you have not demonstrated a process that can be reproduced (i.e., duplicated) by your team. In other words, your business will never grow beyond what you can do by yourself. For the sake of your team, your business, and your sanity, keep it simple. Use the tools.

Not An Invitation to Join

Magic questions are not an invitation to join your company. The prospect doesn't have enough information to give you an answer to that question yet, and it's not fair for you to ask. Remember, prospecting is all about the prospect. Maximize his ability to evaluate your offer properly—one step at a time.

Contents of a Magic Question

The content of your magic question is critical. An effective magic question has two characteristics.

1. Deals with Objections

The best time to deal with objections is before the prospect raises them. The magic question is the best place to deal with the most common objections. A carefully crafted magic question can virtually eliminate one or more objections.

2. Hard to Say "No" to

The philosophy behind the principles of prospecting is to create a low friction conversation. An effective prospecting conversation will prepare the prospect for your magic question. Your magic question, in turn, will minimize any resistance the prospect may have to accepting your offer. In other words, a good magic question will make it difficult for the prospect to say "no".

Make sure your question does not contain words or phrases that are likely to raise a red flag. Here are some phrases to avoid:

- business
- join
- home-based
- ground floor
- part-time
- involved
- extra income
- my wife and I
- opportunity (singular form)
- …you'd be so good…
- …ought to do what I'm doing…

The above phrases are overused and smack of an inexperienced approach. An effective magic question will cause the prospect to believe that it would be risky for him to say "no". At the same time, you want him to realize that saying "yes" is not at all risky.

Delivery

The way you deliver your magic question has direct bearing on how the prospect will receive it. There are three elements to the effective delivery of a magic question: transition, setup, and voice.

1. Transition

One key aspect of delivering a magic question is a smooth transition to the question. It doesn't make sense to have a short conversation and then suddenly blurt out an offer of opportunity. Doing so would be amateurish and completely ineffective. The best way to ensure a smooth transition is to use transition phrases. Later in the book, two principles, *Mental Judo* and *You Let the Dogs Out* (Chapters 10 and 11, respectively) address transitions in detail.

2. Setup

You only get to ask the magic question one time. Make sure you have the prospect's attention before you ask it. You want him paying attention and you want him to know that you expect a response. If you set him up prior to the question, things will work out fine. The example later in this chapter illustrates how to do this.

> *For your information, just answer me one question.*
> —Samuel Goldwyn

3. Voice

An effective magic question will come across as a natural part of the conversation. If the prospect detects a significant shift in the conversation, he will raise his guard. One way to make sure your manner seems natural is to maintain the same voice. Take care to use the same tone, the same volume, and the same cadence (speed) as you ask the question.

It's also important to speak clearly. Generally, you get one shot at delivering the magic question. Don't blow it with poor enunciation. Speak clearly and pace yourself by using strategic pauses. If the prospect is unable to follow you, you're wasting your time. The example below illustrates the use of pauses.

Examples

The text below spells out a magic question that works really well. I use it more often than I do any of the others. This question is generic and works for any opportunity. The commas represent pauses of about a half second each.

Raw Phrase

Jack, let me ask you a question. Are you at all open, to explore outside opportunities, as long as they don't conflict, with what you're already doin?"

Outline

Jack, let me ask you a question[1]: (pause) Are you at all open[2], (pause) to explore[3] outside[4] opportunities[5], (pause) as long as they don't conflict (pause) with what you're already doin'[6]?

Notes

1. The setup — this statement gets the prospect's attention and lets him know that you are expecting a response. (If you don't yet know the prospect's name, start with "Let".)

2. This phrase is a qualifier (aka: a tie-down). If Jack responds with "no", he is admitting that he is closed-minded and would never be open to exploring. This is a risky position for him to take, because he does not yet know what he is saying "no" to.

3. Tells Jack that he would merely be looking, not doing. This is a low risk activity not requiring commitment. (making it easy for him to say "yes")

4. A clue that his participation will be above and beyond his current job or business. It's a way of saying part-time without actually using that phrase.

5. This is the crux of the entire conversation. Notice the use of the plural form. You're not asking if he would be interested in your one and only opportunity. Instead, you're asking if he is open to opportunities in general. This subtle difference dramatically increases the likelihood of Jack accepting your offer.

6. This priceless phrase generally eliminates the objection of "I don't have time." What the prospect hears is "it won't take too much time." With this phrase, you are acknowledging that the prospect is already busy which deals with the time objection before he brings it up. It also deals with the objection "my boss doesn't want me doing anything else." (A less common objection, but the question deals with it automatically).

This magic question has evolved through years of practice. It generates amazing results when delivered correctly as part of a properly developed conversation. This particular magic question does, however, have one distinct disadvantage: it's complex. This makes it harder to memorize, harder to enunciate, and harder to understand. That is why the pauses (and lots of practice) are necessary.

The question above is provided as the first example because it illustrates how an effective magic question can alleviate objections. You may however, get better results when you first start out, by using one of the simpler magic questions listed next.

Other Examples

- Do you look at other ways to make money, if they don't take too much time?
- Are you at a point in life where you would be open to explore outside opportunities?
- Are you making all the money you can stand?
- Do you ever feel like you're worth more than you're getting paid?
- Do you keep your income options open?
- Do you keep your options open?
- Do you ever explore other ways to make money?
- Are you open to exploring additional streams of income?
- Are you open to explore outside options?
- If I could show you a way to double your free time without affecting your income, would we have something to talk about?

The possibilities are endless. As you examine these magic questions, notice that they share several characteristics:

- Above all else, they are questions. You want a yes or no answer, so ask a yes or no question. The person asking the questions controls the conversation.
- They avoid the red flag phrases identified earlier in this chapter.
- They contain different words, but they sound similar. That's because all magic questions have the same basic goal — to find out if the prospect has enough interest to accept your prospecting tool. The subtle differences in wording allow you to tailor your question to the prospect (see *Chameleon of Many Colors,* Chapter 14).

39

chapter Five

What's Your Name, Jack?

Is this the party to whom I am speaking?

—*Ernestine, the Telephone Operator*

(Lily Tomlin on NBC's Laugh-in)

You Don't Know Jack

So far, we've called the prospect "Jack," a fictitious name. When you're prospecting for real, you're going to need a strategy to get the prospect's name that isn't too forward. This chapter describes some strategies to do just that.

You Need to Know Jack

At some point, before the conversation is over, you're going to have to get Jack's name. There are several reasons that knowing his name is important.

1. Who You Gonna Call?

Follow up calls can be a bit awkward when you don't know the name of the person you are calling. What will you say when someone answers? It's much less confusing to ask, "Is this Jack?"

2. It's Music to Their Ears

People love to hear their name. Speaking their name is one way to relate to them. It is one component of good people skills. The key is to use their name without overdoing it. When you use their name as part of every other sentence, it sounds insincere and manipulative. Typically, I will use the prospect's name one or two times.

3. It Fosters Familiarity

Another reason to use the prospect's name is to begin fostering familiarity. The people who know Jack call him Jack. If you call him Jack, you must know him too, right? Of course, you're not fooling anyone. You and Jack just met and both of you know it. It's not about misrepresentation. It's about positioning. You are positioning yourself as someone Jack knows and trusts.

Getting His Name

One way to get Jack's name is to come right out and ask him. This strategy however, is flawed. If you ask a prospect for his name without first sharing yours, he may perceive you as a threat. He may start asking himself (or you) questions like, "What are you going to trying to sell me?" or "I don't know you. Why do you need to know my name?"

You need to earn the right to ask his name. You want it to be natural for him to share his name. Jack should feel comfortable telling you his name. Start out with a peace offering like your own name or friendly small talk. When you apply the principles of prospecting, Jack will be more than willing to share information, including his name.

Here are several points in the conversation that make natural times to ask for the prospect's name:

1. After He Answers the Magic Question

One way to get the prospect's name is to introduce yourself immediately after he answers the magic question. Ordinarily, Jack will reciprocate by introducing himself in return.

Example

Y:	I know this is coming out of left field, but let me ask you a question. Are you open to exploring outside opportunities?
P:	Sure.
Y:	By the way, my name is Russ—Russ McNeil. (as you say it, extend your hand to initiate a handshake)
P:	I'm Jack.
Y:	Like I said, I know we don't know each other, but if I loaned you a DVD* for a couple of days, would you at least take a look?

*Note: some teams use books, magazines, or CD's instead of DVD's.

In this example, you initiate the name exchange immediately after he responds to your magic question. Here's the skinny:

Raw Phrase

By the way, my name is Russ—Russ McNeil.

Outline

By the way[1], my name is Russ[2]—Russ McNeil.[3] (as you say it, extend your hand to initiate a handshake) [4]

Notes

1. A transition phrase

2. Demonstrate goodwill by offering your name first. Use first name only. This makes the exchange more personal. Moreover, it's easier for him to remember a single name.

42

3. Repeat with your full name. This reinforces his memory of your first name and insinuates that he should offer his full name.

4. Never underestimate the power of touch. It draws the prospect further into the overall encounter.

It's alright if he doesn't tell you his last name, but he's going to feel awkward if he doesn't at least state his first name.

Occasionally, the prospect won't offer his name at all. The handshake is your backup plan. If he hasn't offered his name before the handshake, say this during the handshake: "What's your name?" Use a tone of voice that says, "I know you told me, but I didn't understand." Smile as you ask. It is extraordinarily difficult for a prospect to resist offering his name in this scenario.

2. As You Get His Phone Number

Another strategy is to wait and get the prospect's name as part of his contact information after you hand him a prospecting tool. See Chapter 16, *I've Got Your Number, Now* for a thorough description of this strategy.

3. Randomly within a Longer Conversation

This book is about situational prospecting; short conversations that establish interest (or lack thereof) quickly. Occasionally, you'll have the luxury of a longer, more relaxed conversation. In these situations, you can use the underdog approach to get the prospect's name.

Example: ... (you've been engaged in a pleasant conversation for several minutes) ...

Y:	By the way, I guess I owe you an apology.
P:	What for?
Y:	Here we are in the middle of a conversation and I haven't even introduced myself. My name is Russ—Russ McNeil.

This is an example of an "underdog" approach. By apologizing, you are assuming a position of transparency and vulnerability. Underdog approaches endear the prospect to you. This scenario works about 100% of the time. The downside is that most prospecting conversations aren't long enough to employ it.

chapter Six

The Secret Ingredient

You have to force yourself out of a comfort zone and really try to figure out what are the key ingredients, the key skill sets, the key perspectives that are necessary.

—*Steve Case*

Love might make the world go 'round, but it takes duplication to make our business model go 'round. Everything you do should be easy to duplicate. One important aspect of being duplicable is being relatable. Being relatable means making it easy for the prospect to see himself following your example. Being relatable is essential for fruitful prospecting.

When you first approach Jack, he will immediately begin forming opinions about you and your actions. Your appearance, your words, your behavior, and your demeanor all influence his opinions. Jack's opinions are partially (perhaps mostly) complete by the time you ask your magic question.

In His Shoes

The key to successful prospecting is this: Always keep the other person's perspective in mind. The whole reason you're prospecting to begin with is to expand your team, right? Well, why would the prospect want to be part of your team if he can't picture himself doing what you're doing? He won't. Period. End of discussion. Thus, if you want your prospecting efforts to be fruitful, you must honor the prospect's perspective.

Always make it a point to walk a mile in the other person's shoes. This sage advice has two benefits: 1) it ensures that you look at the situation from the prospect's point of view and; 2) if he gets angry because you took his shoes — he's barefoot and you have a mile head start!

The list below outlines some fabulous ways to taint the prospect's perspective. Use of these strategies will ensure a botched prospecting attempt.

- Excessively overdress or underdress
- Show too much excitement
- Share too much detail
- Be too serious or intense
- Offer your opportunity too early in the conversation
- Focus the conversation on *I* instead of *you*
- Make obvious exaggerations

The Ever-present Question

When you offer your opportunity to Jack, he will immediately ask himself a question. He asks this question instinctively, automatically, and sub-consciously. You won't hear him ask it because he also asks it silently. Here is the question he asks, "Can I picture myself doing what this person is doing?" The question may take on a slightly different form such as…

- Am I able to do what this person is doing?
- Am I willing to do what this person is doing?
- Am I willing to do to others what this person is doing to me?

If the answer is yes, the prospect might be interested in accepting your offer of a prospecting tool. If the answer is no, he definitely will not be interested in your offer. To increase your odds, be relatable.

Bad News, Good News

The bad news is that when you are prospecting a stranger, you typically get only one chance to influence his perspective. The good news is that the influence you exert is completely under your control.

All of the information in this book boils down to one basic concept: influencing the prospect's perspective in a positive way. Every phrase, philosophy, and principle sports at least of the following properties, known affectionately as the *Three Cs.*

1. Congenial

Simply put, being congenial means that you are friendly. You're respectful, polite, and pleasant. In short, you're likeable. If people like you, they will want to be around you. They will be more receptive to your message. They will be more likely to buy from you. Being likeable is necessary. Personal development makes it possible.

2. Credible

"You are absolutely incredible!" Wow! What a compliment! Wouldn't you like to hear that more often? Slow down, Turbo. The prefix "in" means not. When it comes to prospecting, you don't want to be *not* credible. On the contrary, you want to be *very* credible. What does being credible have to do with prospecting? Well, if you don't come across as believable, the prospect is not likely to be interested in your offer. A few prospects may recognize that your opportunity is viable even if you aren't — very few. Be believable.

3. Concise

One definition of concise is "free from elaboration and detail." This is of paramount importance while prospecting. If you are sharing details while you're prospecting, you're saying too much. Instead of being the messenger, you are becoming the message itself, which is a colossally bad idea. You run the risk of saying enough for the prospect to say "no", but not enough for him to say "yes". Any story worth telling is worth telling properly. Don't sell yours short by trying to regurgitate it in the span of ninety seconds. Which brings us to the next law:

4th law of prospecting

It is better to use tools than words.

What's the Secret Ingredient?

The secret ingredient is surprisingly simple: *Always keep the prospect's perspective in mind.* Don't say anything without first considering how the prospect will perceive your words. Don't do anything without first evaluating how he will perceive your actions.

A good place to start with your evaluation is to consider how you would feel if Jack prospected you the same way that you are prospecting him. What would you think? How would you look at the experience? In essence, the secret ingredient is another way of expressing The Golden Rule: "Do unto others as you would have them do unto you." The difference is, that as a professional prospector, you will not only *do unto,* but you will also *speak unto.*

> *The Golden Rule is of no use to you whatever unless you realize it's **your** move.*
>
> —Frank Crane

When you approach, you are creating an entire experience for the prospect. This experience has within it, the potential to change the lives of people you have never met. Moreover, you have the awesome responsibility of constructing this experience all by yourself. You don't have to be the world's best prospector. You just have to be the best you. By adding the secret ingredient to your prospecting recipe, you're light years ahead of most reps.

Specific Examples

The eighth principle, **Chameleon of Many Colors,** describes how to adapt your style to the style of the prospect. For now, just concentrate on how the prospect will perceive the overall prospecting experience.

Speak Unto ...

If you're prospecting an executive, don't ask, "Hey dude, would you like to make some extra money?" Conversely, if you're prospecting the waiter at your favorite restaurant, you shouldn't say, "Have you ever considered the potential leverage of diversifying into multiple ongoing revenue streams?" These are extreme examples, but they illustrate the absurdity of talking in a way that won't relate to the prospect. Make sure your words relate to the audience.

Do Unto ...

If the prospect is soft-spoken and laid-back, you need to recognize that he is probably a mild-mannered person by nature. Think about how he will perceive you if you're bouncing around like your hair's on fire, using sweeping hand gestures, and bellowing every word like a megaphone with oversized batteries. Be sensitive to his perspective and behave accordingly. Make sure your performance relates to the audience.

The U's Have It

The Secret Ingredient mandates that you keep the prospect's perspective in mind. The corollary to this idea is realizing that prospecting is not about you. It doesn't matter how you want to act, how you want to talk, how you want to dress. The fifth law of prospecting is quite clear about this:

5th law of prospecting

It's not ever, ever, *ever* about you.

Ask not what the prospect can do for you, but what you can do for the prospect. Focus on what your product can do for Jack, not how much commission you'll earn if he buys it. Offer your opportunity to Jack so his wife can be a full-time mom, not so you'll move to the next pin level.

The word prospect does not contain the letter "I." Don't attempt to add one. As a rule, avoid saying "I" as you prospect. Instead, focus on the word "you." This is almost automatic when you ask questions instead of making statements. The few times a statement is more appropriate than a question, consider saying "we" instead of "I," such as in the examples below:

Instead of this...	Say this...
I have some information you ought to look at.	Are you open to exploring outside opportunities?
I know you're going to like what you see on the DVD.	There's one part in particular that's the most popular. Is a couple of days enough time for you to check it out?
I recommend that you look at this DVD.	If you like what you see, we can sit down and fill in the gaps.

Lest you think that the secret ingredient is some ambiguous idea, keep in mind that you are still learning background material. You will discover that when you apply the principles of prospecting, the Secret Ingredient gets added to the recipe automatically. Keep reading, the "Aha!" moments are about to begin.

principle number **One**

Put a Funnel in His Ear

No man would listen to you talk if he didn't know it
was his turn next.

—*E.W. Howe*

Concept

Imagine the conversation between you and the prospect as having the shape of a funnel. It is broad (more general) at the beginning and narrow (more specific) at the end.

What's in a Name?

Have you ever seen a television or movie character using a funnel as an improvised hearing aid? I remember at least two such characters. This makeshift use of a funnel inspired the name of the first principle, **Put a Funnel in His Ear.**

Description

Of the eight principles described in this book, seven of them are concrete. That is to say, they describe specific actions, words, and attitudes to use while prospecting. In contrast, **Put a Funnel in His Ear** is abstract. Rather than suggest specific words or actions, it provides an outline of the overall conversation.

It is only an outline because too much detail would be restrictive and thus useless. There is no way to anticipate exactly how any one conversation will unfold. Having an outline for the conversation will help you to keep the conversation

I never let my subject get in the way of what I want to talk about.

—Mark Victor Hansen

focused. Another reason for using this particular outline is that it can help you get to the point quickly (and naturally), which is necessary for prospecting moving targets.

Parts of the Funnel

The funnel has three parts: the opening line, the main conversation, and the magic question.

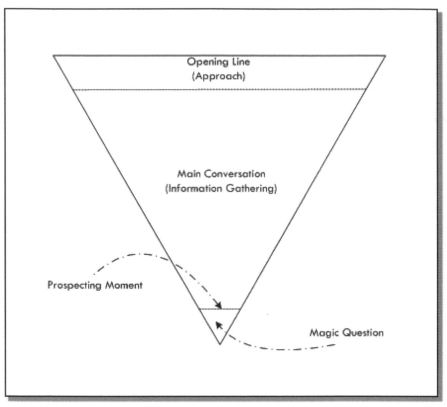

Figure 4: The Conversation Funnel

1. Opening line

Once you have engaged the prospect by speaking the opening line, you have put a funnel in his ear. The wide opening of the funnel represents the fact that you have a number of opening lines at your disposal. The wider your variety of opening lines, the easier it will be for you to seize various prospecting opportunities. As soon as the prospect responds positively to your opening line, you move straight to the next part of the funnel.

2. Main conversation

This is the bulk of the conversation. There are several goals to achieve during this part of the conversation.

Put the Prospect at Ease

Everyone is his own favorite subject. That's why most people are comfortable talking about themselves. A common theme throughout *PROSPECTING POWER!* is keeping the prospect in his comfort zone. By talking about a familiar subject, the prospect is less likely to raise his guard. This reason alone is enough keep the conversation focused on him.

Collect Useful Information

A second aspect of the funnel is that of collecting useful information. The more you know about the prospect, the more likely you will detect a need or desire that your opportunity can fill. The most important information to gather is about the prospect's occupation. What he does, how long he's been doing it, and what organization he works for, all are important facts to collect. A later principle, **Curiosity Paid the Cat** (Chapter 9), explains how to get this information in a natural and non-threatening manner.

Apply the Information

Collecting information from the prospect is one thing. Applying it is quite another. Keep in mind that you just met the prospect. Suggesting that you have a specific answer to all of his problems (or even one of them) may come across as arrogant or presumptuous. This will not win points with him. There is a time and a place to explain how your opportunity can address the prospect's need. Be aware that for many prospects, the first encounter is not the time or the place.

One way to use the information is to form a connection with the prospect. **Curiosity Paid the Cat** (Chapter 9) covers this subject in detail, so we will explain it fully in that chapter.

Another way to use the information is to customize your lead-in to the magic question. For example, pretend that the information you gather includes the fact that the prospect is a financial planner. You may decide to customize your lead-in to be something like this:

You know, I heard another successful financial planner speak a while back. He shared something interesting. He said that in his experience most people should consider developing a second stream of income. Does that sound like good advice to you?

There is no requirement to use the gathered information directly so if a connection does not already exist, don't fabricate one.

3. Magic Question

By collecting the appropriate information in the proper manner, you justify the magic question. This is the final goal of the funnel and it is more subtle than the previous ones. For the longest time, I was completely oblivious to this benefit. Now that I am aware of it, I realize it is a powerful aspect of the conversation funnel.

If you get answers to the correct questions, the prospect will be allowing you a small, brief peek into his life. By transitioning smoothly from the body of the conversation to the magic question, the prospect may assume that the two are connected. In other words, the prospect might assume that you are asking the magic question because of some of the information he just finished sharing.

The last thing you want is the prospect thinking is that you make a habit of having the same conversation with everyone. If the prospect believes you are offering something based on his particular circumstances, he will: a) feel more special, and b) be less likely to ask, "Why are you asking me?"

This concept of justifying the magic question occurs on a subconscious level making it both powerful and irresistible.

Pulling the Plug

> *He, who builds a fence, fences out more than he fences in.*
>
> —Turkish proverb

From time to time, the prospect simply will not cooperate. Maybe Jack insists on answering your questions with one-word responses. Maybe his facial expressions make it clear that he is not comfortable talking to you. On rare occasions, you may run into a real cynic that will actually ask a question like, "What are you selling?" or "Why are you asking so many questions?" The principles in this book will dramatically reduce the likelihood of negative responses. Even so, you should be prepared to respond appropriately when it does happen.

Keep in mind, that you have the cookie. You are offering to introduce Jack to a fantastic opportunity, to train him, and to invest your time in him all at little or no cost to him. Chances are no one else in his life is making such an offer. In short, you are offering him a gift. If Jack chooses to decline the gift, it is his loss, not yours.

If he responds negatively, your best course of action is to "pull the plug." Bow out of the conversation. The key is to bow out with grace and composure. You should terminate the prospecting process knowing that you did the right thing with your heart in the right place. The rule here is to remove any reason for regret.

One way to end the conversation is simply to quit talking. This is the best course of action if the prospect is responding with short or gruff answers. Just zip it up and go on about your business (perhaps looking for another prospect to engage).

If the prospect turns cynical, respond confidently and then drop the conversation. The primary goal in this situation is for you keep your head high. A distant secondary goal is for the prospect to spend the rest of the day wondering what he missed. Your response should be something that fits your personality. Here are some of my personal favorites:

Example 1

P:	What are you selling?
Y:	What am I selling? What kind of question is that?

When you deliver this line, your expression and your tone of voice should say, *I can't believe you're asking me that.* After your response, go about your business and disengage from the conversation.

Example 2

P:	Why are you asking so many questions?
Y:	I guess I'm just curious. I didn't mean to offend anyone.

Say this line in an overtly upbeat tone almost as if he was joking. Then drop the conversation.

chapter **Eight**

principle number **Two**

100% Chance of Sunshine

Wherever you go, no matter what the weather, always bring
your own sunshine.

—Anthony J. D'Angelo

Concept

Conduct yourself in a way that makes everyone glad to meet you.

What's in a Name?

Isn't is odd how weather forecasts always seem so negative? "There is a 20% chance of rain tonight and a 40% chance of thunderstorms tomorrow." That sounds so gloomy and pessimistic. It seems to me that instead of "20% chance of rain," it would sound more upbeat to say, "80% chance of sunshine." The second principle, *100% Chance of Sunshine,* owes its name to this positive-rather-than-negative outlook.

Description

What exactly is "sunshine" referring to and how can you go about creating it? In this context, sunshine refers to a genuinely upbeat attitude. When you leave after meeting someone, that

> *Some cause happiness* **where***ver they go; others* **when***ever they go.*
>
> —Oscar Wilde

person should feel great about your visit or encounter. The world we live in constantly bombards us with negativity. Be positive in a genuine way, and you will stand out like an oasis in the desert.

You may represent the only pleasant interaction the prospect has all day. Suppose he works in a negative environment. His co-workers are always complaining, his supervisor is a jerk, he is working more hours than ever before, and his company has frozen wages for a year and half. Now suppose that you meet the prospect at random in line at a restaurant. You are enthusiastic about life, you find some small way to compliment him, and you show a genuine, albeit brief, interest in him. Do you suppose that he will remember your conversation? Do you think he might be open to looking at your opportunity? You had better believe it. He might even assume that your upbeat attitude is a direct result of the opportunity you are offering (and he's probably right). Of course, he wants to know more.

It's The Right Thing to Do

Ideally, you will incorporate this principle into the very fabric of your life. Make it part of your SOP, your standard operating procedure.

Any time you interact with a person, drop a little sunshine into his life. You may not even intend to prospect that specific person. Whether or not you intend to prospect the person is irrelevant. Shine on them any way. Being positive does not mean that you go over the top and act happy to the point of being obnoxious. All you have to do is be the type of person that *you* would want to be around. Practice *100% Chance of Sunshine* because it's the right thing to do, not because you have an agenda.

It Makes Your Job Easier

You may be thinking, "That's all well and good for some people, but what you're suggesting just isn't my style." If so, ask yourself this: "Do I really want to build a large team?" If you do, then keep in mind that the sixth law of prospecting is non-negotiable.

6th law of prospecting

Positive attracts. Negative repels.

If you don't consider yourself a positive person, know this: You can change. (Back to personal development as mentioned in *Magic of Conditioning*).

> *Weather forecast for tonight: dark. Continued dark overnight, with widely scattered light by morning.*
>
> —George Carlin

Becoming the type of person that continually shines on others will make you naturally attractive to others. The more attractive you are to others, the easier it will be to prospect for your business. *100% Chance of Sunshine* is the right thing to do and it's working smart. How many reasons do you need? Go scatter some light.

With Respect to Manners

Treat all of your acquaintances with respect. Something as trivial as displaying good manners like:

- Yes, sir
- No, ma'am
- Please
- No, thank you

> *Manners are one of the greatest engines of influence ever given to man.*
> —Richard Whately

… is an excellent way to demonstrate respect. This idea isn't exactly rocket science, but it is a great way to get the conversation off the launch pad.

Sometimes the simplest measures can make a significant impact. Show the same respect to all people regardless of age, culture, or occupation. The less respect Jack gets from others, the more he will appreciate the respect he receives from you.

Use Humor

Humor is a great way to brighten a person's day. In the words of one of my mentors, "If you can make them laugh, you can make them buy." And make no mistake; prospecting does involve selling. In this principle, you are selling the fact that talking to you is a positive experience and more importantly, one worth repeating.

Humor is not something easily taught. In some ways, it is easier to explain what to avoid. For some people, humor comes naturally. For others, being humorous is simply not in the genes. The use of humor is optional so don't force it. No humor at all, is always better than poorly executed humor.

> *The best humor combines professional, friendly, and funny.*
> —Jeffrey Gitomer

Avoid Jokes

Do not tell jokes! You have no idea what sensitivities the prospect may have (e.g., political, occupational). Don't run the risk of offending him. Besides, your idea of funny may be completely different from the prospect's idea of funny. Another reason to avoid jokes is that the joke you are thinking of, may take too long to tell. The final reason to avoid jokes is that you might just stink at telling jokes.

Avoid Sarcasm

Sarcasm is a negative form of humor. Usually, someone is on the receiving end of sarcasm. The object of this principle is to build up, not tear down. Don't use destructive humor.

Humor That Works

Here are some guidelines for effective humor in prospecting:

- Keep it light. Belly laughs are not the goal.
- Aim the humor at the conversation or situation, never at the prospect.
- Poke some fun at yourself.
- Make unexpected responses or off-the-wall observations.

Example

It's morning and you're at a coffee shop. The person at the register rings up your order and tells you the total is $2.89. Look at him with an expression of total surprise and say, "That's strange. It only cost $2.88 yesterday." Keep the serious look on your face long enough for him to realize he has absolutely no explanation. Then grin ever so slightly.

This is an example of a humor grenade; the blast can hit several people in the vicinity. In fact, you might be speaking to the person behind the counter, but if you hear the sharp-looking executive behind you chuckle, you may decide to prospect him, too.

Be Complimentary

If your mom told you once, she told you a thousand times, "If you don't have something nice to say, then don't say anything at all." Well, *100% Chance of Sunshine* takes this idea one step further. This principle calls for you to go out of your way and look for nice things to say.

Nothing will brighten a person's day like a compliment. Nothing flags you as a phony faster than fawning or flattery. Be sincere and genuine. Being complimentary is a skill that you can develop. It is simply a matter of practice.

There are three types of compliments.

1. Direct Compliments

A direct compliment is one where you use words to say something nice about the prospect.

Examples:

- This restaurant always seems to runs so smoothly. You must be an awesome manager.
- You seem so underutilized in this job. What's your degree in?

> *Be a people people.*
> —K. Townes

Notice that both examples involve making an assumption. We assumed that the prospect is the manager and we assumed that the prospect has a degree. Take the first example. If you are correct and the prospect is the restaurant manager, he feels complimented that you recognized that fact. If he is not the manager, he feels complimented that you recognize that he is capable of the position. Either way you delivered a compliment directly to the prospect.

Gender Benders

Consider asking permission before paying direct compliments to someone of the opposite gender (e.g., "May I pay you a compliment? ... That dress is definitely your color.") This will enhance the sincerity of your question and preclude any question about your true intentions.

2. Indirect Compliments

An indirect compliment is a compliment that you pay to the prospect while talking about something other than the prospect. This downplays the compliment, which, ironically, gives it more impact.

Examples:

- As a recruiter for a fast growing company, I'm always on the lookout for sharp people like you who know how to carry a conversation. How long have you worked here?

- Someone with a great personality like yours is worth a lot of money to the right company. They must be paying you really well.

Notice how these compliments are followed immediately with another statement or question. When you convey an indirect compliment, do not wait and pause until a sentence or two later. This enhances the sincerity of your compliment, making it more effective.

3. Associative Compliments

An associative compliment is a compliment paid to something associated with the prospect rather than the prospect himself.

Examples:

- I need a tie that color. Can I have yours?
- What a beautiful car. Would you like to trade?

Associative compliments are the easiest type of compliment to deliver, they rarely cause the prospect to question your motives, and they make excellent conversation starters. These particular examples also incorporate a bit of humor. These may seem silly, but try them before you rule them out.

Make it a Habit

Note: the name of the principle is *100% Chance of Sunshine,* not 80% or even 99%. Make a habit of being positive. That way, you will begin to attract prospects naturally. Attracting people is a lot easier than chasing them. Trust me; I've tried both.

Next, learn how asking questions can pay huge dividends.

I. Thou shalt prepare thyself through personal development

II. Thou shalt not pressure the prospect

III. Thou shalt keep the prospect's perspective as thine own

IV. Thou shalt ask questions and not make statements

V. Thou shalt be pleasant, positive, and professional

VI. Thou shalt be relatable in all thine actions

VII. Thou shalt realize that sowing comes before reaping and that reaping comes only in due season

VIII. Thou shalt not commit information regurgitation

IX. Thou shalt trust in thine prospecting tools

X. Thou shalt follow-up with purpose and in a timely manner

The Ten Commandments of Prospecting

chapter **Nine**

principle number **Three**

Curiosity Paid the Cat

Curiosity is the very basis of education and if you tell me that curiosity killed the cat, I say only that the cat died nobly.
— *Arnold Edinborough*

Concept

While you're talking to Jack, be curious and ask good questions. Take care to remember key information about his occupation. Then use the collected information in future conversations with both Jack and future prospects.

What's in a Name?

No doubt, you've heard that curiosity killed the cat. When it comes to prospecting, just the opposite is true. In this industry, controlled curiosity can cause copious cash to accumulate in your accounts.

Description

Being curious and asking the right questions can pay huge dividends in both the long term and the short term. Gathering useful information is the essence of *Curiosity Paid the Cat.*

To FORM or not to FORM

You may be familiar with the FORM model of conversation. FORM is an acronym:

Family

Occupation

Recreation

Message

The FORM model of conversation suggests that the elements of family, occupation, recreation, and message are a logical progression of conversation. The thought being that, if asked, a person is generally willing to talk about his family. From there, additional questions can lead the conversation to his occupation and eventually to what he likes to do for fun (recreation). By this point in the conversation, you have discussed three subjects that he is comfortable with so the two of you should be relating well. In essence, you have primed the person to receive your message (which was your ultimate goal all along).

FORM is okay when you're prospecting stationary targets over the course of several encounters, but it takes too much time to be useful with moving targets. The principles of prospecting still apply even when you use FORM. The two are not mutually exclusive.

Waste No Time

When you're prospecting a moving target, you have to be able to engage the prospect, relate to the prospect, gather information from the prospect, and make an offer to the prospect—all in the span of one to two minutes. You don't have time to learn his life history.

You need a small number of questions that get the information you need. The most useful information you can gather from the prospect is about his occupation. There are three questions in particular that pay the cat.

As you study the questions below, keep in mind that by the time you ask them, you've already made a positive first impression with *100% Chance of Sunshine* (Chapter 8). Show a little finesse. You don't want Jack to feel interrogated. You're participating in a conversation, not presiding over an inquisition.

Question 1: "Work around here?"

Ask this question in an ultra casual tone, as if it were small talk with no particular purpose. As you speak, put the emphasis on the word "work." This question is not grammatically correct. Don't sweat it. If you were concerned about proper grammar, you would ask, "Do you work nearby?" You're not interested in correct grammar. What you want is results! By omitting the words "Do you," the question is less direct and thus less threatening. It also projects a more casual style of conversation. Think about how you would ask about the weather (e.g., "Think it's gonna rain?").

This question is non-threatening and the prospect will generally answer it with no resistance. You don't care if he says "yes" or "no". You just want an answer.

Set His Frame of Mind

One purpose of this question is to cause the prospect to think about his occupation. Forcing the prospect into a "work" frame of mind will prepare him for the second question.

Set a Precedent

The second purpose behind this question is to set a crucial precedent in the conversation: You ask a question, the prospect answers. You will rely on this precedent throughout the conversation. With the question, "Work around here?" you have entered the body of the conversation funnel (see *Put a Funnel in His Ear,* Chapter 7).

Set the Appointment

The final purpose behind this question is that the answer may come in handy setting an appointment as part of the follow up. Ultimately, when a prospect accepts a prospecting tool, you will call to follow up. If he expresses interests at that point, it may make sense to arrange a face-to-face visit. If you already know where he works, you can suggest a meeting location near his place of work *(Follow Up or Fall Down,* Chapter 17).

Question 2: "What do you do professionally?"

Of all the questions you ask during the prospecting conversation, only the magic question is more significant than this one. Knowing the prospect's occupation is pivotal to the remainder of the conversation.

> *A single question can be more influential than a thousand statements.*
>
> —Bo Bennett

Ask this question immediately after the prospect answers the first one. You don't want to sound rushed, but you don't want to hesitate either. Make it sound like you're asking this question because of how he answered the first one. There are several distinct benefits of getting an answer to this question.

His Favorite Subject

An obvious benefit is that of encouraging Jack to talk about himself (which of course, is his all-time favorite subject). Since his job is probably a significant part of his life, it makes a great subject to talk about.

Justify the Magic Question

Another benefit of asking Jack about his occupation is that it will help to justify the magic question. This is an abstract benefit and it often operates on a subconscious level. Here's how it works: One minute Jack is talking about his occupation; the next, you ask your magic question. He may assume that you're asking because of what you just learned about his occupation. This assumption may be conscious or subconscious. Either one makes Jack more receptive to your offer.

A Direct Connection

Curiosity was framed.
Ignorance killed the cat.

—Unknown

Yet another benefit of discovering the prospect's occupation is that you may be able to establish a direct connection between the prospect's occupation and your opportunity. For example, if you or someone on your team (aka upline, downline) has the same occupation as the prospect, you might use this coincidence as a reason to offer your opportunity.

An Indirect Connection

The final benefit of asking about the prospect's occupation is more esoteric—it may provide a basis for an indirect connection to the prospect. For example, consider this dialogue excerpt:

Y:	Work around here?
P:	Yeah, a couple miles back that way.
Y:	What do you do professionally?
P:	I'm a travel agent.
Y:	Really. How long you been doin' that?
P:	About 8 years.
Y:	**You know...I met a guy a while back who was also a professional in the travel industry.** I wish I had kept his business card. Do you have one on you?

Look at the bold text. When you mention meeting someone else that shares Jack's occupation, you solidify a connection with Jack. It's almost as if you said, "Really. I used to be a travel agent." Notice also, the indirect compliment "also a professional." We connect with, and compliment the prospect all in the same breath. This is a fine example of how the principles combine to complement one another.

To capitalize on this benefit, collect information on the occupations of everyone you prospect or visit with. Over time, you will develop an extensive list of occupations. The bigger your list, the easier it is to develop an indirect connection. Take care that you do not force this. Sincerity is king. If occupation does not provide a genuine connection, don't fabricate one.

Question 3: "Really. How long you been doin' that?"

The third and final question is easy for you to ask and easy for the prospect to answer. It's also easy to underestimate its benefits.

"Really" Really Works

For the longest time, I was completely unaware of how I had incorporated the word "really" into my prospecting conversations. One day, I went to lunch with one of my reps and as we were leaving the restaurant, I successfully prospected a total stranger. Afterward, the other IBO remarked how much he liked how I used the word "really." He was especially intrigued at how it seemed to cause the prospect to open up to the rest of the conversation. Because of his observation, I began to analyze my use of the word "really." In particular, I needed to know how I was saying it and why it seemed to work so well.

The first thing I realized is that when I would say "really," I was not asking a question. I was making a statement. As you say the word, drag it out a bit like this: reeeel-ly. Enunciate the first syllable with rising inflection and the second syllable with falling inflection. When you get it right, magic occurs. Here's why: the sound that comes out of your mouth is *reeeel-ly*, but what the prospect hears is, "Oh my goodness! I have been looking for a person who does that!"

The second thing I realized is that "really" serves as a transition phrase. It encourages the prospect to believe that this question is a result of how he answered the previous one.

Another reason for using this particular transition phrase is that it demonstrates interest in what the prospect has to say.

When you combine the correct inflection with a casual tone, you orchestrate a dialogue that is natural and spontaneous. The last thing you want is for the prospect to feel like you're interrogating him.

The Prospect's Perspective

Originally, I would ask this question to learn where the prospect is on the timeline of his career. Here is an assumption that is relatively safe to make: The longer Jack has been in his career, the more likely he will be willing to look at something else. Conversely, it may be hard for your opportunity to compete with the enthusiasm Jack has about a new job he recently started. Keep in mind, that you should not use these generalizations to pre-judge his interest. Instead, use them it to understand his perspective *(The Secret Ingredient,* Chapter 6).

Easy Does It

There is another benefit of asking this particular question: It is completely non-threatening. Asking this question softens the previous one. It tells the prospect

> *When someone says, "That's a good question," you can be sure that it's a lot better than the answer you're going to get.*
>
> —Franklin P. Jones

(subconsciously, of course) that the hard questions are over. This in turn, will soften his defenses. Do not underestimate the power of this subtle concept.

Controlling the Conversation

The previous sections describe the benefits of asking three highly specific questions that pay the cat. There is another benefit derived from asking questions in general. The very act of asking questions will produce this other benefit no matter what the questions are. This additional benefit is not merely a fact—it's the law...

7th law of prospecting
He who asks the questions controls the conversation.

Common rules of conversation will compel the prospect to answer your questions. In fact, ignoring your questions would be downright rude. When you ask Jack a question, he has a choice to make — answer your question or be rude. Once you develop the skill of asking strategic questions in a non-threatening manner, you will have complete control of the conversation.

Remember that you are the one driving the conversation. The prospect does not know what you are going to say next. Consequently, you can talk about whatever you want to. Since you get to pick the subject, choose wisely.

Once you gather the correct information, you are ready to begin transitioning to the magic question. The next chapter, *Mental Judo,* shows you how.

chapter **Ten**

principle number **Four**

Mental Judo

Thus the principle of judo, from the beginning, is not one of aggression, but of flowing with things.

—*Carl Becker*

Concept

Use the prospect's thoughts to influence his perception of you and your offer.

What's in a Name?

I'm not an expert in the martial arts, but there's one thing I know about judo. Judo uses an opponent's momentum to throw him around by redirecting his movement. In this principle, *Mental Judo,* you will learn how to use the prospect's own thoughts to redirect his perception and gain his confidence.

Description

Chances are the term judo conjures up thoughts of two or more opponents engaged in a stylistic physical contest where the participants take turn slamming each other to the ground. Have no fear. Neither of you are going to be tossed around (at least not physically) and no one is going to get hurt. In fact, don't think of prospecting conversations as combat at all. Regardless of the outcome, no one is going to lose. The literal translation of judo is "gentle way"—a perfect picture of the current principle.

Best of Breed

If I had to pick one principle over all the rest, it would be this one. Of all the principles, it is the simplest to master and the most influential. Be careful where you point this stuff. It really packs a punch.

Being Relatable

The better you relate to Jack, the more attracted he will be to your offer. The most effective way to relate to him is to demonstrate that you share some of the same thoughts. You want Jack to sense that you and he think alike. By saying what Jack is thinking, you will secure a strong connection with him. When the prospect hears you speak his own thoughts, he will perceive you as an ally, not a threat. This subtle, gentle influence is the essence of *Mental Judo.*

Put Yourself in the Prospect's Position

So how can you know what the prospect is thinking? That's easy. Think about how you would feel if you were in his position. A total stranger strikes up a conversation with you. The inquisitive stranger asks a few questions. Then the stranger offers an invitation to some vague opportunity. That's a lot of strangeness. The stranger does not know you. He has not earned your trust. On what basis does he offer anything? His offer seems to come completely out of left field. And *that* is precisely what the prospect is thinking. Your offer is coming out of left field. Another expression that comes to mind is "right out of the blue." If you were the prospect, isn't that what you'd be thinking?

Say What the Prospect is Thinking

If you can say what the prospect is thinking, you're close to getting a response from him. Because...how can he resist? You're on his wavelength. You've hit the nail on the head. You and he are partners in a single thought.

—G.F. Brown, *Advertising for Results*

The key to *Mental Judo* is saying what the prospect is thinking *before* he thinks it. To one degree or another, all prospects will be thinking the same thing (i.e., "left field," "out of the blue"). Knowing this gives you a huge advantage. You know what he will be thinking after you ask the magic question so right before you ask, speak his thoughts.

Shifting the Prospect's Perception

Properly applied *Mental Judo* will cause a shift in the prospect's perception. This shift takes place on a subconscious level and the effects are dramatic. Without *Mental Judo,* the prospect may very well perceive you and your offer as a threat. With *Mental Judo,* he will perceive you as a friend and your offer as a treat.

Golden Gate Bridge

Mental Judo sports another benefit as well. It serves as an effective bridge in the conversation. If you went from information gathering (the main conversation of the funnel) directly to the magic question (at the bottom of the funnel), the conversation might seem incongruous, choppy, unnatural. *Mental Judo* forms a smooth transition between these two phases of the conversation.

Examples

Let's say you have a prospect engaged in the conversation funnel. You've collected some valuable information and now you're ready to pose the magic question. How do you transition the conversation to the subject of opportunity? Try this:

By the way, Jack, *I realize this is coming out of left field,* but let me ask you a question. Do you ever explore other ways to make money if they don't take too much time?

Here's another one:

By the way Jack, *I realize we just met and we don't know each other from Adam,* but I just have to ask you a question: Are you at a point in life where you'd be open to look at additional sources of income?

Let's look at one more. This time we'll dissect the paragraph into its component phrases to get a better understanding of the psychology involved.

Raw Phrase

By the way, Jack, *I know this is coming completely out of the blue,* but based on our conversation, I feel like I just have to ask. Are you at all open to explore outside opportunities as long as they don't conflict with anything you're already doin'?

Outline

By the way, Jack[1], *I know this is coming completely out of the blue[2],* but based on our conversation[3], I feel like I just have to ask[4]. Are you at all open to explore outside opportunities as long as they don't conflict with anything you're already doin'[5]?

Notes

1. This phrase transitions from the main conversation of the funnel (Chapter 7) to the magic question (Chapter 4).

2. The core *Mental Judo* phrase; speak his thoughts, builds rapport

3. Justifies your offer; prevents the prospect from asking "why me?" Only use this if you are prepared to back it up with a legitimate rationale. This phrase is optional (the first example didn't include it).

4. Setup for the magic question

5. The magic question (not part of *Mental Judo*)

Try it, You'll Like It

"Ouch" is not a judo term.

—Neil Ohlenkamp

Right about now, you may be thinking, "Russ, you can't possibly be serious – *'We don't know each other from Adam'*? Surely you don't actually say that to the prospect." I sure do and it works great. The suggested phrases, *"... from Adam," "... out of the blue,"* and *"... left field"* may not represent the way you normally express yourself. Nonetheless, you can be sure it's what the prospect is thinking. So, if you don't like these, find a similar phrase you do like and use it. Once you try it, you'll understand.

Thank You, Lieutenant Columbo

Mental Judo is so effective that brand new reps can become prospecting machines by using this one principle all by itself.

If you're like many new reps, you occasionally find yourself talking to a stranger that you want to prospect. The conversation is pleasant enough and you even have a prospecting tool nearby. The challenge is that you spend most of the conversation trying to figure out how to bring up the subject of opportunity. Rather than listening to Jack, your mind is running in circles. When you do blurt out something about opportunity, your offer seems out of place.

Here's an idea I teach new reps. It's simple and it works great. If you get nothing else out of this book, take this idea and experiment with it. I call it the Columbo approach[1]. It works like this:

- You're talking to someone you don't know.
- Have a natural conversation.
- Don't talk about your opportunity.
- Don't even think about your opportunity.
- Focus on the conversation, be a good listener.

Let the conversation run its natural course. At some point, you will turn to leave. Immediately after you turn away from Jack, turn back to face him (or his back if he has turned away also) and say this:

By the way Jack, (pause) is it okay if I ask you a question? (Jack will say yes) I know this is coming out of left field, but I was wondering, are you at a point in life where you'd be open to look at outside opportunities?

The important part of this technique is postponing the magic question, turning away, and then turning back. The specific magic question you use is irrelevant to the technique. *Caution: Don't try this unless you have a prospecting tool nearby because you're going to need it.*

> *Learn from the mistakes of others. You may not live long enough to make them all yourself.*
>
> —Admiral Hyman Rickover

At this point, you're halfway through the eight principles. Four more and we'll tie them all together. In the next chapter, you'll learn how to draw the prospect into your offer by inviting him to decline. What? Can that really work? You had better believe it. Moreover, it's a lot of fun. Keep reading.

---

[1] Named after Lieutenant Columbo, the TV detective. He was famous for questioning a suspect then after turning to leave, he would turn back to the suspect and say "Just one more question…" His final question would be a real zinger, one the suspect never saw coming.

chapter **Eleven**

principle number **Five**

You Let the Dogs Out

A dog in desperation will leap over a wall.
—*Chinese proverb*

Concept

Give the prospect an obvious opportunity to decline your offer. If the prospect gets the impression you are backing him into a corner, he will not respond favorably. Show him an open door through which he can exit.

What's in a Name?

A while back, there was a popular, albeit short-lived, song titled *Who Let the Dogs Out?* The title of this song inspired the name of the current principle. When it comes to prospecting, we know exactly who let the dogs out — you did! You let them out every time you leave the back door open.

Description

You Let the Dogs Out means giving Jack a way out that he can easily identify. To let the dogs out, the open door must be obvious to the prospect. It only counts if Jack can see that he isn't cornered. Be explicit. If he doesn't realize that you've left him a way out, he may feel trapped. There is more to leaving a door open than simply not pressuring him. Omitting pressure is a passive measure and covered in the next chapter. Leaving a door open, on the other hand, is an active measure. More specifically, it is something you say.

The psychology of this principle works opposite the way you might think. The easier it is for the prospect to "escape" the conversation, the more likely it is that he will accept your offer.

Good for Both Parties

Letting the dogs out is good for the prospect and it's good for you. For starters, it sets the right tone. Proper team building hinges on trust and cooperation. By giving the prospect an obvious way out, you are demonstrating trustworthiness. If you corner the prospect, the implication is that your offer is one-sided. If that is the perception you create, you have lost him already. Even if he doesn't physically move away from you, he will check out mentally. Instead of *Who Let the Dogs Out?*, you'll be singing *Oh Where Has My Little Dog Gone?*

 Keep in mind that you don't want to sponsor a person who isn't legitimately interested. If you have to drag a person *into* your business kicking and screaming, you will have to drag him *through* it kicking and screaming. If you provide the prospect an exit and he chooses to walk through it, let him go! You are in the sorting business, not the convincing business. Sort the prospects into two groups: 1) the ones who want to look at your prospecting tools, and 2) the ones who do not. As you might have guessed, this too is a law.

8th law of prospecting

Amateurs convince. Professionals sort.

Changing a negative perception

The idea of your industry may be a turn-off for Jack. Perhaps there's another IBO in his life who doesn't know when to shut up. By providing an obvious way out, you are demonstrating a refreshing professionalism that can help reverse a negative perception. If your approach is refreshing enough, he might not associate your opportunity with Network-Marketing at all (which means you can start with a clean slate). Talk about refreshing.

Examples

Consider a scenario where:

- You made an approach
- You asked a few good questions
- You are ready to ask the magic question

Now say something like this:

Jack, let me ask you a question. I know this is coming out of left field so **let me know if I'm barking up the wrong tree,** but do you keep your income options open?

Here's an alternative:

Raw Phrase

Jack, let me ask you something. I know that we just met, so **let me know if I'm off base. OK?** Do you ever look at other ways to make money if they don't take too much time?

Outline

Jack, let me ask you something[1]. I know that we just met[2], so **let me know if I'm off base[3]. OK[4]?** (wait for response) Do you ever look at other ways to make money if they don't take too much time[5]?

1. This is a transition. It also makes sure you have Jack's attention. Otherwise, *You Let the Dogs Out* might be wasted.

2. Throw in a little bit of *Mental Judo* for good measure.

3. This one little phrase gives Jack permission to turn down your offer if he so chooses. You both know he doesn't need your permission to decline. By giving him permission anyway, you are demonstrating goodwill; you are showing him that you're not trying to corner him. You have left the back door wide open. This is the core *You Let the Dogs Out* phrase.

4. Another question will help you maintain control. In this instance, you're securing Jack's buy-in. Be sure to wait for his response.

5. This is the magic question. It's not part of *You Let the Dogs Out.*

When you skillfully apply this principle, it becomes an open admission that your offer may not be relevant to him. The mere suggestion that he may not have any interest, removes all pressure. Congratulations. A relaxed prospect is a willing prospect. Where will you take him next?

Now you know how to keep the prospect relaxed by actively showing him a way out. Next, you will learn how to relieve any apprehension he already had by passively portraying an attitude of nonchalance.

chapter **Twelve**

principle number **Six**

Feeding the Birds

The bird of paradise alights only upon the hand that does not grasp.
—*John Berry,* Flight of White Crows

Concept

Move slowly through the prospecting encounter and avoid being too aggressive or forward. Otherwise, you may spook him.

What's in a Name?

Imagine that you go to a park to feed the birds. The birds love bread so you bring along a full loaf. As you near the area where the birds are gathered, you consider the best way to approach them.

Would you charge into the flock like a vendor at a ball game barking "FRESH BREAD! FRESH BREAD! GET YOUR FRESH BREAD HERE!" No, of course you wouldn't. That would surely scare them away.

A more sensible tactic would be to enter the area quietly and calmly. You might even approach at an indirect angle instead of walking directly toward them. You would drop the bread in small pieces until the birds realize that you represent a treat, not a threat. In so doing, you attract the birds. They realize that you have something they want, and they move closer to you.

Description

Feeding The Birds reminds us to attract the prospect, not attack him. There are three aspects to this principle:

1. How you physically approach the prospect;
2. How you verbally approach the prospect;
3. How you verbally approach the subject of opportunity;

Approach the prospect and the subject of opportunity indirectly. Help the prospect realize that you have something he may want. Just like feeding the birds.

See Jack Run

Have you ever gone to a shopping mall for the sole purpose of meeting prospects? So have I. How well did it work for you? That doesn't mean there's anything wrong with prospecting at malls. More than likely, it's how you went about it.

How did you dress? Did you wear Sunday clothes on Saturday afternoon? Were you carrying a stack of prospecting tools such as magazines or DVD's? Did you boldly walk up to a total stranger and immediately start offering one of your tools (that you just so happen to have a stack of)? I've done all of these things before, but not any more.

Let's look at the experience from the perspective of the prospect. Pretend you're the prospect…

There you are minding your own business, casually strolling on the upper level of the mall. Your mind is a thousand miles away so you don't realize the man in a business suit is walking directly toward you. He is smiling as he steps up and says "hi," but this does little to stifle your surprise. You're caught completely off guard so you miss the first few seconds of what he says. The next thing you know, he is shoving a DVD in your face. Should you thank him or run the opposite direction? In your confusion, you compromise by accepting the DVD and saying nothing. As if that's not strange enough, this total stranger then has the audacity to ask for your phone number. That's not just strange, that's downright threatening. You give him a phone number. As you hurriedly make up a reason to get away from him, you take comfort from the fact that he'll never call. You know this because the number you gave him — it isn't yours.

The point of this illustration is not to discourage you from prospecting at malls. The point of the illustration is to make you aware that your approach determines your reception. The quality of your approach has tremendous influence over the prospect's perception of your offer.

Anytime Jack evaluates an opportunity, the number one question he will ask himself is this: "Can I see myself doing what this person is doing?" (*The Secret Ingredient,* Chapter 6). Jack must be able and willing to do what he sees you do. If not, he's out of there. Run Jack, run.

Tuxedo or Toga?

When I first started learning about our industry, one of the things I kept hearing about was appropriate business attire. The predominant message was "dress a cut above." I assumed that if a "cut" above were good, then several cuts above would be even better. Consequently, I instituted a new personal dress code: suit and tie for all occasions, zero tolerance.

Big mistake.

You never know when you may bump into a great prospect, so you want to stay prepared. To that end, it's important to dress sharp, but it's even more important to dress in context. Dressing in context means this: Dress appropriately for the activity you have planned. If you are on your way to an appointment with a successful executive, wearing a suit and tie makes sense. Conversely, if you're destination is the car wash, a suit is absurdly out of context.

When you dress out of context, you are less relatable. I have found that the best way to dress is in context. When you know ahead of time that you will be in a particular prospect-rich environment, plan to dress one cut above the norm for that setting. If cutoffs are the norm, wear tailored shorts or casual slacks. If sport coats and button-down shirts are the norm, wear a tie.

The Physical Approach

If you begin the encounter close enough to start a conversation, the physical approach is already complete. The rest of this section assumes that you are not yet within range of conversation.

When you zero in on a prospect and walk directly toward him, and he sees you, he will quickly start wondering about your intentions. The more distance you have to cover in your approach, the more defensive he will become. The more energy he sees you expending to move toward him, the more serious he will assume your purpose is. (That's not a good thing, as you will see in the next chapter, **Casualize & Minimize**).

It's preferable to find some other reason for moving closer to the prospect (e.g., to admire his car, to reach for a nearby personal development book, or to check out the lime leisure suit you that caught your eye). Use this reason as an excuse to move into range of the prospect.

The Verbal Approach

Having moved close enough for conversation, you are ready to make contact (Chapter 3). For example, if your excuse for moving closer is to:

- Admire his car: Offer a compliment. *(100% Chance of Sunshine)*
- Reach for a personal development book: ask him to recommend a good book. Can you think of a better kind of person to prospect? *(Magic of Conditioning)*
- Check out that lime leisure suit: Seize the occasion for some light humor. *(100% Chance of Sunshine)*
  - Ask the prospect: Do you think this makes my butt look big?
  - Ask the prospect: Do you have any idea how long I've been looking for this color?
  - Hold the suit up, look at it, raise the volume of your voice slightly, and say to it: Aha! I finally found you!

Author's Note: Just to set the record straight, I'm only kidding about the lime leisure suit (if it was a serious example, the suit would be orange). The purpose of the leisure suit comments is to demonstrate how unexpected humor can both lower Jack's defenses and start a conversation. You may be thinking, Russ, those examples aren't even funny. Maybe not, but let me assure you of one thing: Jack will not have his guard up.

Getting Around to Opportunity

Once you have made successful physical and verbal approaches, you have entered the conversation funnel *(Put a Funnel in His Ear)* and you are on your way.

Be Patient

If you jump directly to the subject of opportunity, you might as well be yelling *"FRESH BREAD!"* Bye-bye, birdie. I heard one trainer refer to such behavior as "going straight for the prospect's jugular vein." You're not from Transylvania and cheap vampire impressions will get you nowhere. Biting Jack on the neck is highly discouraged. You lose points and the prospect loses pints.

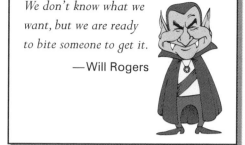

We don't know what we want, but we are ready to bite someone to get it.
—Will Rogers

Keep Jack relaxed by keeping the conversation cordial and natural. Wait and ask the magic question at the end of the conversation almost like an afterthought.

Introduce Doubt

Feeding the Birds is not entirely about your attitude or style. It's also about your words. It's about taking time and moving gingerly through the conversation so as not to spook the prospect. Here are some verbal strategies that can help keep the birds at ease:

Consider a scenario where you already…

- made an approach
- asked a few good questions
- asked your magic question and gotten a positive response
- put a prospecting tool in his hand

Now say something like this:

Jack, it's real simple. Check out the disc. **If you like what you see,** we'll get together and fill in the gaps.

The emphasized phrase illustrates *Feeding The Birds.* The word "if" introduces doubt. By introducing doubt, you are trailing the bread behind you. The prospect knows he may not be interested and you are agreeing with him. You and Jack are seeing eye-to-eye. For an alternative with more impact, try this:

Jack, it's real simple. Check out the disc. **If there's any common interest,** we'll get together and fill in the gaps.

Like the previous phrase, this phrase also tells the prospect that he may not be interested in your offering. Then it goes a step farther by telling him that *you* may not be interested in *him*. The experienced IBO will recognize this as a light take-away. Think of it as negative pressure, also known as a vacuum. You know what a vacuum does — it attracts unfastened objects. If the prospect is still having doubts up to this point, he may suddenly become more attracted to your offer.

The effect of introducing doubt is powerful, but subtle; and subtlety is the essence of good prospecting. Even so, these phrases are optional, so don't think you have to force them into every conversation.

The purpose of **Feeding the Birds** is to keep the prospect from raising his guard as you approach him. Next, you will learn how to keep the prospect relaxed after you ask the magic question.

Gender Benders

The examples in this chapter introduce the notion of getting back to the prospect. At this point in the conversation, it's easy to spook prospects of the opposite gender. Even if the prospects are comfortable with you, they may have concerns about how their spouse will react. One way to mitigate these concerns is to include the spouse in your statement. For example:

Jill, this is real simple. If you like the magazine, maybe I can visit with you and your husband to fill in the gaps. If you don't find it interesting, that's okay too. Does that sound fair?

Assume that prospects of the opposite gender are married. It's okay to be wrong. By making the offer to meet with both of them, you are demonstrating professionalism. You address a potentially significant issue right up front but you did it without blowing the issue out of proportion.

"Success in our business is about the 80/20 rule. Like showing 10 and sponsoring 2. In the process of building your business you may find that for every 20 people who say yes, there are 80 who say no. But the good news is, if you will continue to be persistent you will become very successful."

—Ron Puryear

Every "no" brings you a step closer to a "yes." Every "yes" brings you a step closer to your goal. You don't care if the prospect says "yes" or "no." Either way, you move forward.

chapter **Thirteen**

principle number **Seven**

Casualize[1] & Minimize

Make everything as simple as possible, but not simpler.
—*Albert Einstein*

Concept

Keep the conversation simple and informal.

Description

A common thread woven throughout all of the *PROSPECTING POWER!*, is that of keeping the prospect's guard down. One way to do this is by keeping the conversation simple and casual. Simple and casual are relaxing, and a relaxed prospect is a willing prospect.

The effects produced by this principle are particularly valuable when applied after the magic question. Of the eight principles, I would pick *Casualize[1] & Minimize* as having the second biggest impact on prospecting conversations.

Speak Casually

In general, people are more comfortable being casual than they are being formal. Given a choice, most men would rather wear blue jeans than

> *It is better to be casual than to be a perfectionist.*
> —Chinese proverb

a tuxedo. Most women, given a choice, would favor tennis shoes over stilettos. We are also more comfortable in a casual conversation than we are having a formal one. It takes more work to speak formally and it's not natural for most of us. If you want the prospect to be comfortable, then speak in a casual, natural manner.

One way to portray casual speech is to replace formal words and phrases with informal ones. The following table offers a few suggestions:

---

[1] Yeah, yeah. I know. "Casualize" isn't really a word, but it has two things going for it: 1) it has a laid back ring to it, making it a perfect fit for the principle itself, and 2) it rhymes with minimize. (My editor says if I include this footnote, then I can leave the word in.)

Replace...	With...
Have a meeting	Get together for a half a cup of coffee
An appointment	A short visit
Check your schedule	Compare calendars
Discuss the details	Fill in the gaps
Presentation	Quick overview
Information	Info

Send the Right Signals

By being casual, you are sending some strong signals to the prospect.

First, you are telling him that you don't take yourself too seriously. A serious tone implies serious consequences, a big red flag to the prospect. This alone could set off his alarms. If so, you have lost him already. Have a nice day.

The second signal you send by being casual, tells Jack that you are comfortable with your subject. If *you* are comfortable, *he* is more likely to be comfortable. This is a good thing. Don't worry; be happy.

The third and last signal you send by being casual is it that you don't care if Jack is interested in your offer or not. Of course, you would like him to be interested, but if he perceives you as nonchalant, he will be more attracted to your offer.

Trivial Pursuit

Another aspect of **Casualize & Minimize** is that of openly trivializing your offer. **Read the preceding sentence closely.** It does not say that you are trivializing your opportunity. If your opportunity were trivial, you would not be involved in it, much less prospecting strangers for it. What it says, is that you will be trivializing your offer.

If the prospect perceives that your offer entails a major decision, he will not be interested. By minimizing the significance of your offer, you're communicating to Jack that he's not making a major decision.

Your goal is to trivialize it to the point that the thought of making a decision never even occurs to the prospect. The phrase "no big deal" is tremendously effective in achieving this goal.

Example

Let's say that you just popped the magic question and offered one of your DVD's to Jack. Let's say also that he accepts the disc and agrees to check it out. What do you say next? Without **Casualize & Minimize,** your next statement might be something like this:

Take that home and study the information on the disc. Afterwards, we can check our schedules and set an appointment so I can meet with you to discuss all of the details.

Here is another way of saying the same thing; this time applying the principle of **Casualize & Minimize:**

Jack, this is real simple. Check out the info on the disc. If you like what you see, we'll visit over half a cup of coffee and fill in the gaps. If you don't, it's no big deal—at least you know one more thing you're not interested in.

Read each one several times. Notice the difference in tone. Put yourself in the prospect's shoes. Which one sounds less daunting? The second one has more words (49 *vs.* 32), but it's more natural and conversational. Not only that, it also screams "risk free" without using the words "risk" or "free." This is the essence of **Casualize & Minimize.**

Let's take a closer look at the phrase above. This time we'll examine how the specific words influence the prospect's perception:

Raw Phrase

Jack, this is real simple. Check out the info on the disc. If you like what you see, we'll visit over half a cup of coffee and fill in the gaps. If you don't, it's no big deal—at least you know one more thing you're not interested in.

Outline

Jack[1], this is real simple[2]. Check out the info[3] on the disc. If[4] you like what you see, we'll [5] visit over half[6] a cup of coffee and fill in the gaps. If you don't[7], it's no big deal [8] — at least you'll know one more thing you're not interested in[9, 10].

Notes

1. Use his name. People love to hear their name spoken.

2. Reinforce the notion that what you're doing isn't complicated.

3. Use "info" rather than "information." Informal speech is highly relatable.

4. Introduce doubt; unassuming, lowers risk. *(Feeding the Birds)*

5. Plants the thought seeds of a partnership.

6. This implies a short amount of time, low risk, and minimal time commitment to participate.

7. More doubt...less risk.

8. You don't care if they come on board or not; you're not going to chase them — how refreshing.

9. This phrase goes beyond reducing risk for Jack. It even goes so far as to state a benefit he will gain by viewing the disc. If he watches it and isn't interested, it will be because the information on the disc didn't appeal to him. In other words, his rationale for saying "no" is contained on the disc itself. On a subconscious level, Jack is thinking that if he does decide to say "no" after viewing, he can put the blame on the disc. This can be important to people that don't like to say "no."

10. Another purpose behind the final sentence is that of openly giving Jack permission to say "no." This is a superb example of *You Let the Dogs Out.*

When you examine this phrase closely, you'll realize that it simultaneously employs three of the principles:

- *Casualize & Minimize* (informal)

- *Feeding the Birds* (introducing doubt)

- *You Let the Dogs Out* (leaving Jack an obvious way out)

Keep practicing. Unconscious competence is a powerful place to be.

One thing that you *don't* see in this phrase is the word "I." Proper prospecting focuses on the prospect not the prospector. Your choice of words should reflect this mindset.

It Is What It Is

The words you say and the tone you use have a dramatic effect on the prospect's perception. Think about gravity for a moment. If a cat falls from a rooftop what will happen? It will fall. Does the cat know about gravity? No. Will gravity have the same effect anyway? Yes. The principle of gravity is in effect whether the object is aware of gravity or not. It is the same way with the principle of *Casualize & Minimize.* If you are uptight, formal, and dramatic you may very well lose the prospect, even if you are completely unaware of why. (Perhaps I should say, *especially* if you are unaware.)

When you first step out and begin to prospect strangers, it is normal to be tense, but your goal is to sound natural. Before you can sound natural, you must get the point where prospecting feels natural. The only way for that to happen is to practice. Naturally.

Now, you know how your verbal communication can help keep the prospect relaxed. The next, and final principle, describes how to use non-verbal communications to enhance rapport even more.

principle number **Eight**

Chameleon of Many Colors

The chameleon changes color to match the earth. The
earth does not change color to match the chameleon.
                                    —*Senegalese proverb*

Author's Note: This chapter is primarily for readers who already have experience prospecting strangers. Some inexperienced readers may feel overwhelmed by the more advanced nature of its subject matter. While this principle can elevate existing prospecting skills to an entirely new level, one can still get great results without it. Feel free to postpone this chapter for now and come back to it after you gain experience with the other seven principles.

Concept

Encourage the prospect to see you as being just like him. If he sees that you and he are alike, you will have more influence over the outcome of the encounter.

What's in a Name?

A chameleon is a lizard-like reptile that relies on camouflage for self-defense. Chameleons change their colors to match their current surroundings. They live successfully by continuously changing color to mimic their environment. The final principle, **Chameleon of Many Colors,** calls for you to succeed at prospecting by "camouflaging" yourself to match the prospect.

Description

Rapport is the most important aspect of effective communication. When you achieve rapport, there exists, on a subconscious level, a feeling of "This person is just like me. I want to understand what they have to say." The more rapport you build with the prospect, the more influence you will have over the encounter.

> *Rapport is the ability to enter someone else's world, to make him feel that you understand him, that you have a strong common bond. It's the ability to go fully from your map of the world to his map of the world. It's the essence of successful communication.*
>
> —Anthony Robbins

It doesn't take long to establish rapport. It is possible to achieve significant rapport in just a few minutes. Keep in mind though, that when you're prospecting moving targets, you don't usually have minutes. Sometimes, you will have only seconds. Does that mean that rapport isn't possible when prospecting moving targets? No, it means that you should build as much rapport as time allows.

Be Responsible

This chapter introduces some strategies that are exceedingly efficient at building rapport. By mastering them, you will be able to influence the conversations of your choice. This influence can be dramatic. Use it responsibly. Wholesome prospecting is not about price, product, or your personal profit. Proper prospecting is about promoting positive progress for the prospect.

---

ma·nip·u·la·tion *(n)*, successfully encouraging Jack to act in a way that benefits *you*

in·flu·ence *(n)*, successfully encouraging Jack to act in a way that benefits *him*

Learn influence. Unlearn manipulation. Be responsible.

Take Responsibility

Do you believe in your product? Do you believe your opportunity can improve Jack's life? Then share it with him. A good way to do that is to meet him where he is. A better way is to become him. Obviously, you can't literally become Jack, but you can temporarily adopt his mannerisms, speech patterns, and thought processes. Doing so will encourage Jack to think of you as being just like him.

You might be asking, *"Doesn't that make me a fraud?"* That is the wrong question. What you should be asking is this: *"Do I believe in my product? Do I believe that my opportunity can improve Jack's life?"* If your offer is good for Jack, then you should make it as easy as possible for him to evaluate it open-mindedly. If you have the ability to make it easier for him, and you don't, you are doing him a disservice. You are an ambassador for your company. It's your responsibility to be your best. Take responsibility.

Matching the Prospect

The cornerstone of **Chameleon of Many Colors** is learning to match the prospect. There are three aspects to matching a prospect:

- Matching his speech patterns
- Matching his physical posture
- Matching his behavioral style

You may choose to match a prospect in any combination of these areas.

Keeping it light

Some of the information in this chapter represents basic NLP concepts. NLP stands for Neuro-Linguistic Programming. There are numerous applications for this sophisticated and well-documented subject. Building rapport is only one of many such applications. What follows is a brief introduction to some basic NLP strategies that you can use to build rapport rapidly.

> I had help with the following two sections, *Matching Speech Patterns and Matching Physical Movements*. In fact, I had a lot of help. I can't say enough about **Penny Tompkins and James Lawley of The Development Company.** They have been extremely generous with their original work, some of which is included in this chapter. Penny and James are true experts in the field of NLP. If you have any interest in learning more about this fascinating subject, I recommend that you visit their web site, www.cleanlanguage.co.uk.

1. Matching Speech Patterns

Of the three matching strategies proposed in **Chameleon of Many Colors,** this one is the simplest.

We all structure our experience of the world through the senses—seeing, hearing, feeling, etc. It goes without saying that you're aware of your external senses, but did you know that you also have a parallel set of internal senses? The following examples illustrate **external senses** used in verbal expression:

Spoken Statement	Sense
I *see* the DVD you're holding	Visual
I *hear* what you're saying	Auditory
I *feel* this magazine in my hands	Kinesthetic

You use the same senses to represent what you are thinking about internally. These following examples show how we use our **internal senses** in our thoughts:

Internal Thought	Sense
Imagining a picture of your mother's face	Visual
Recalling a conversation you had yesterday	Auditory
Remembering a time you felt powerful and motivated	Kinesthetic

When you use your internal senses, you are in essence, creating your "mind's eye." The words you say to yourself affect emotions such as joy or enthusiasm, which in turn affect your behavior and mood. The words that Jack uses reflect whether he is thinking with his visual, auditory, or kinesthetic systems. This gives you an insight into how his brain is sorting information at the time. You can't tell *what* Jack is thinking but you can have a good idea *how* he is thinking—and *that*, is precisely what you want to match when you're prospecting him.

You can have a good idea how Jack is thinking if you pay attention to the words he is using. The following table identifies some common word clues.

Using the Word Clues

When you know to listen for the types of words Jack is using, you can know what sense he is using when he's thinking. You can in turn, use this knowledge to

Visual	Auditory	Kinesthetic
imagine	talk over	walk through
see	listen	heavy
show	tune in	pass over
colorful	loud	touch upon
illustrate	call	get a hold of
insight	resonate	feel
picture	hear	numb
look	sound	kick around

create a deep rapport thereby influencing the prospecting encounter on a subconscious level.

Everyone uses all of the internal senses to some degree; but one or two are likely to predominate. For instance, if Jack is visually oriented, he is more apt to see pictures in his mind's eye. He will use words like those in the Visual column above. If Jack's auditory sense is strongest, his internal dialogue will contain more words like "hear," "listen," and "speak."

If you keep using auditory words to a visually oriented prospect, he will have to translate from your senses to his own. This unconscious translation takes time and can be difficult for some people. The more difficult the translation for Jack, the more your rapport will be inhibited.

Listen for the sense words that indicate how Jack is thinking. Then adjust your communication style to match. In other words, when you talk to Jack, use the same sense words that you observe him using. In so doing, the chameleon matches the prospect's speech patterns. It's that simple.

2. Matching Physical Movements

You may already have some familiarity with this concept. It is commonly referred to as mirroring and matching.

Mirroring

Mirroring is a term used to describe the process of duplicating the prospect's physical behaviors. Behaviors you can mirror include:

- Body Posture
- Hand Gestures
- Facial Expressions
- Weight Shifts
- Breathing
- Movement of Feet
- Eye Movements

Mirroring is physically copying Jack's behaviors in an effort to reflect his movements back to him. You are pacing his experience, and although he may be unaware of your mirroring, it will still have a profound effect. On a subconscious level, Jack feels acknowledged and appreciates your interest in him.

When you first begin to practice mirroring, try it with just one aspect of the prospect's physical behavior, perhaps his posture. Once you get the hang of it, gently include another behavior such as hand gestures. Over time, add additional behaviors until you find yourself mirroring without thinking about it. The more you practice, the easier it will become.

When you mirror, always do so respectfully and with subtlety. Mirroring done with integrity and respect creates positive responses (in you as well as in Jack). Otherwise, mirroring becomes mimicry and produces negative results. As you develop your rapport skills, remember to base the powerful effect you create on honorable values and proper principles.

Matching

Matching is very similar to mirroring. The primary difference between the two is timing. While mirroring is simultaneous with the prospect's movements, matching typically exhibits a time delay. For example, if someone is gesturing while talking and making a point, you should remain still and be attentive. When it is your turn to speak, you can make your comments and your point using the same or similar gestures.

You will find that you hear and observe other people in more detail as you learn the skills of mirroring and matching. Paying attention to others in this way is a process of building trust, and the more elegantly you mirror and match, the more your prospects will turn into "raving followers."

3. Matching Behavioral Style

There are billions of people on this planet and yet there are only four basic personality traits (dominance, influence, steadiness, conscientiousness). What makes us all different is the fact that each of us represents a unique blend of these four traits.

A number of models have been developed to describe the personality types. Even among top industry trainers, multiple models are used. This book uses four colors to represent the four basic personality types. In my experience, the colors model is one of the simplest to grasp and the most widely taught within the context of Network-Marketing and Direct-Sales. The table below shows how some of the other common models relate to the colors.

Trait	Colors	DISC	Greek	Animals
Dominance	Red	D	Choleric	Lion/Shark
Influence	Blue	I	Sanguine	Otter/Dolphin
Steadiness	Yellow	S	Phlegmatic	Retriever/Whale
Conscientiousness	Green	C	Melancholy	Beaver/Sea Urchin

Why It's Important

So, who cares about all this personality stuff? You do! Here's why: Virtually everything about your behavior—how you express yourself, how you perceive new ideas, how you approach problems, how you relate to others (including strangers), etc., is governed by your personality. And guess what? Nearly everything about the way Jack behaves is governed by *his* personality. By understanding the colors you will be able to match the prospect's personality and style. Remember the chameleon.

Who the Heck Are You?

Your personality represents a blend of the four traits, but not necessarily in equal parts. More than likely, one of the four is predominant over the other three. This is your "primary color." It is imperative that you determine your colors so you can take inventory of your natural strengths and weaknesses. Read the short descriptions below to get some idea of your primary color.

There is one important idea to keep in mind as you read and apply information regarding behavioral styles. No matter how you choose to represent the four basic traits (colors, DISC, animals, etc.), you are not categorizing or labeling the prospect. Doing so would be unfair to the prospect and counterproductive to your goal. You are merely using these devices as tools to help you relate and communicate more effectively.

Red (dominance)

Domineering, fast-paced, decisive, bossy, opinionated, take control, goal driven, success motivated, willing to say "no," impatient, fearless, likes to delegate, unafraid to debate, values the mission over the people involved, task-oriented, extrovert. Symbol: Reds will shoot first (bang!) and aim later. !¹ makes an apt symbol of this personality.

---

¹ Using !, ★, ±, and ? to symbolize the basic personality types is a registered trademark of Dr. Robert A. Rohm, Ph.D., founder of Personality Insights, Inc. They are used here with permission. Visit his web site (www.personality-insights.com) to learn more about DISC and why he chose these particular symbols.

Blue (influence)

Influential (able to talk you into anything), funny, likes to start new projects but rarely completes them, easy-going, smiles and laughs a lot, enjoys being center of attention, prone to exaggerate, skips around in conversation, speaks before thinking, thrives on recognition, oblivious to details, people-oriented, extrovert. Symbol: Blues love to get recognized, so we give them a shiny star: ★ [1]

Yellow (steadiness)

Slow and steady, resistant to change, difficulty saying "no," avoids conflict, easily spooked, values relationships, passive aggressive, needs of others are top priority, takes orders well, people oriented, introvert. Symbol: Yellows won't make waves. They just go with the flow. Think of this when you see ± . [1]

Green (conscientiousness)

Methodical, detail-oriented, cautious, skeptical, cynical, perfectionist, thorough, prone to over-analyze, sensible, practical, unemotional, cold, values correctness over people, task-oriented, introvert. Greens are curious and skeptical. They question everything. The obvious symbol for them is: ?

You can probably ascertain your primary color from the preceding descriptions. For a free online evaluation of your personal color blend, visit www.AhaUniversity.com.

I Once was Color Blind, But Now I See

Right after I began my MLM career, a mentor recommended that I read a book. Not just any book, but a specific book that he suggested would help me build my team fast. The book

> *My recruiting is in full color.*
> —Paul J. Meyer
> a recruiting affirmation

turned out to be about the four personality types. I haven't been the same since. You see, our personality influences *all* of our behaviors, not just our business-related behaviors. Once I began to apply this newfound knowledge, I became not only a more efficient team builder, but I also improved in my role as spouse, father, business owner, manager, and employee. In short, I became a better human being.

Once you know your own colors and understand how they relate to the other ones, you have a powerful tool at your disposal. When you learn how to ascertain the prospect's primary color up front, you have an advantage before the conversation even gets started. As a student of the colors, you will know where Jack's hot buttons are and how to press them. Even more important, you will know where his warning buttons are and how to avoid pressing them.

Each of the following four sections addresses one of the colors. Read them to learn clues that can help you quickly ascertain a prospect's primary color. Learn things to do (and not to do) in the name of building rapport. Each color section ends with a style-tailored phrase that encourages the prospect to explore your prospecting tool right away.

Author's Note: As you study the clues in the following sections, keep in mind that these clues have some caveats attached. 1.) They are not the result of scientific study, but rather informal observations I have made through my own experience. 2.) They are merely guidelines—stereotypes. They are surprisingly accurate, but stereotypes nonetheless. 3.) Occasionally, the clues will be wrong. Stay flexible throughout the encounter. As the conversation progresses, be prepared to "change" your colors rapidly.

Red Prospects
- Confident, fast-paced, bottom-line oriented, abrupt, impatient

Visual Clues
- Large, powerful cars (e.g., faster varieties of Mercedes, BMW, Cadillac)
- Purposeful walking style: head up, hurried pace
- Sharp, crisp attire; women wear low heels so they can look successful and still walk fast.
- Big gestures; leaning forward
- Nodding head before the other person completes a statement

Verbal Clues

- Speaking in absolutes (e.g., "never," "always," "will not")
- Action words (e.g., "do," "take," "control," "perform")
- Abrupt, interrupting, completing others' sentences

Other Clues

- Display of impatience (especially toward slow or incompetent people)
- Willingness to confront (e.g., not letting others break into line)
- Willing to break rules (breaking in line themselves)

Relating to Reds

- Focus on "what" — market trends, potential, etc.
- Project confidence — Reds respect strength and disdain weakness. Make sure you come across confident and secure. If you don't gain his respect, you won't get his attention.
- Get to the point — Reds assimilate information rapidly. Don't use ten words when five will suffice. Reds know where they're going. If you ramble, he will assume that you don't have a clue where you're going. Know what you want to say and get it said.
- Move with a purpose — Reds are constantly on a mission. They have places to go and things to do. If you seem lackadaisical, he won't relate to you.
- Acknowledge his success — Reds are goal-oriented. If you find a way to recognize his success, you can win some major points. One way to do this is through compliments *(100% Chance of Sunshine)*.
- Appeal to his sense of leadership — Reds are leaders and they know it. For example, after you find out the nature of his occupation, you might say something like this: "A while back, I met another project manager. It seems to me that it would take strong leadership skills to be successful at that. How long have you been doing it?" *(Curiosity Paid the Cat)*
- Respect his independence — Reds like to give orders, but they don't take them very well. Never tell Reds what to do or not to do (unless you want to have him do just the opposite). For example, if you hand Jack a DVD and then say, "Now Jack, make sure you watch this tonight," he may never watch it just to prove that he's in control.
- Don't laugh too much — A little light humor is OK but if you overdo it, Reds may not take you seriously.

Finishing in Red Style

Once Jack accepts your prospecting tool, you might say something like this:

Jack, the information on that disc **gets to the bottom line in a hurry.** If you like what you see, we'll visit over half a cup of coffee to see if there's any real common interest. If not, no big deal. Does that sound fair?

Look closely at the phrase in bold type. Both "bottom line" and "hurry" speak directly to the Red psyche. This is an example of how to change your colors to match the prospect. As you can see, it's only a minor shift in the wording. Often, minor differences make the difference between good prospecting and great prospecting.

Blue Prospects

- Friendly, outgoing, boisterous, amusing, unfocused, disorganized

Visual Clues
- Convertible cars (so everyone can see them wave)
- Easily distracted by other people, including strangers
- Brightly colored clothes
- Exaggerated facial expressions
- Friendly, open posture

Verbal Clues
- Excessive exaggerations
- Loud talking (and lots of it)
- Laughter comes easy and often

Other Clues
- Enjoy being center of attention
- May start the conversation before you do

Relating to Blues
- Focus on "who"—emphasize the people (e.g., the ones you're teamed with, the ones you want to introduce them to)
- Be friendly—Blue personalities like people and they especially like people who like them. A friendly expression might win him over at the beginning of the encounter.

- Laugh with him, show interest in him—this demonstrates your appreciation for Jack. The Blue style thrives on appreciation.
- Have fun, be excited—Blues love to have fun. Laugh and joke a little. Smile a lot. If he sees you having fun, he will want to join the party. If he believes he's missing all the excitement, he'll practically ask you to sign him up on the spot!
- Emphasize recognition—this is the number one hot button for Blues. Be careful that you don't share too much detail trying to explain the recognition.
- Avoid detail–the Blue personality is not interested in details. In fact, he may be completely unaware that they even exist! Don't enlighten him.

Finishing in Blue Style

Once Jack accepts your prospecting tool, you might say something like this:

Jack, just wait 'till you see the **people** on that DVD. You're gonna have a blast seeing how much **recognition** they're getting. If you like what you see, we'll visit over half a cup of coffee to see if there's any common interest. If not, no big deal. That's fair isn't it?

Here's a fun alternative:

Jack, that DVD is a lot of fun. Who knows — **you might even see someone you recognize!** If you like what you see, we'll visit over half a cup of coffee to see if there's any common interest. If not, no big deal. That's fair isn't it?

Yellow Prospects

- Mild-mannered, considerate, people pleasing, easily intimidated, resist change and new ideas

Visual Clues
- Gentle gestures
- Slow and steady movement, general lack of urgency
- Overt consideration of others
- Recognize Yellow by ruling out Red, Blue, and Green

Verbal Clues
- Prefers listening over talking
- Warm tones
- Slow-paced

Other Clues

- They avoid the limelight
- Easily embarrassed
- Compelled to follow rules

Relating to Yellows...

- Focus on "how"—how you appreciate the team spirit, how well the team works together
- Be sincere—Sincerity is a big deal to Yellows
- Be gentle—Yellows spook easily and are slow to accept new ideas. Move and speak slowly. Keep inflection and expressions mild. Portray excitement in what you say (words), not in how you say it (tone). *(Feeding the Birds)*
- Be warm—Yellows won't care how much you know until they know how much you care.

Finishing in Yellow Style

Once Jack accepts your prospecting tool, you might say something like this:

Raw Phrase

Jack, can **I count on you** to take a look at that DVD sometime over the next two days? (wait for response) Great. If you like what you see, we'll visit over half a cup of coffee and I'll show you how we focus on teamwork. Sound good?

Outline

Jack, can I count on you[1] to take a look at that DVD sometime over the next two days?[2] (wait for response)[3] Great. If you like what you see, we'll visit over half a cup of coffee and I'll show you how[4] our[5] team[6] focuses on helping people[7]. Sound good?

Notes

1. As a Yellow, Jack is a people-pleaser. He will not want to let you down.
2. This implies that beyond two days, he has let you down.
3. Wait for Jack to "buy in."
4. "How" is important to Yellows
5. The use of "our" is purposefully ambiguous. Does it include Jack? Let his subconscious decide.

6. "Team" denotes a spirit of cooperation. Yellows like the idea of mutual support.

7. "Helping people" and people-pleasing go hand-in-hand

Green Prospects

- Cautious, thorough, accurate, cold, curious, skeptical

Visual Clues

- Automobile: economical, reliable, safe cars
- Clothing: earth tones, pressed, starched, impeccably coordinated
- Standoffish posture

Verbal Clues

- Precise, monotone speech
- Superfluous details (e.g., "1:30 last Tuesday" instead of "last week")
- Seldom laughs

Other Clues

- Fact-oriented
- Gestures are controlled, unemotional

Relating to Greens

- Focus on "why" — (e.g., why it makes sense to check out a tool, why you're making an offer to him)
- Be credible — Don't exaggerate. As a Green, Jack wants hard, cold facts from a source he can trust. If you don't seem credible, you'll lose him.
- Approach slowly (physically and conversationally) — Initially, the Green will not trust you. Don't validate his skepticism by mounting a frontal assault.
- Honor his personal space — Make sure there's plenty of personal space between you and a Green prospect. Keep your body turned at a slight angle so that you do not face him squarely.
- Make no attempt at humor — He won't joke around with you. Return the favor.

Finishing with Green Style

Once Jack accepts your prospecting tool, you might say something like this:

Raw Phrase

Jack, there's a lot of information on that DVD. Make a list of questions and I'll touch base in a couple of days to see if we can get you some quality answers. Does that sound logical?

Outline

Jack, there's a lot of information[1] on that DVD. Make a list[2] of any questions you may have[3] and I'll touch base in a couple of days to see if we can get you some quality answers[4]. Does that sound logical?

Notes

1. The Green wants information. Let him know that that's what he'll find on the disc.

2. Greens love to make lists.

3. He will have questions. Greens always have questions. By acknowledging this fact, you are being more relatable.

4. Notice that this example leaves out the "visit over half a cup of coffee" remark. You are a new acquaintance and the Green will need some time to warm up to you. Suggesting a face-to-face visit before he has more information may seem premature to him. A face-to-face is still your intent, but you may not want to broach the subject in the first encounter (wait until the follow up call).

No matter how good you are at building rapport, eventually you're going to encounter prospects that have questions of their own. In the next chapter, you will learn about responding when the prospect asks *you* questions.

"I argue very well. Ask any of my remaining friends. I can win an argument on any topic, against any opponent. People know this, and steer clear of me at parties. Often, as a sign of their great respect, they don't even invite me."

—Dave Barry

If you're a published pundit like Dave Barry, this phrase is priceless. If you're a professional prospector, it's poison.

chapter Fifteen

The Most Dreaded Question

Don't ask so many questions and they will all be answered.
—*Michael Dorris,* A Yellow Raft in Blue Water

There is one question dreaded by inexperienced reps from all companies. This question is dreaded because 1) it is so common and 2) less seasoned reps are not sure they have a good answer. You may already know the Most Dreaded Question (MDQ). Just to make sure we're on the same page, I'll spell it out. The MDQ is, "What is it?"

It's simple enough to look at. It sounds innocent when spoken. What's the big deal? After all, it's only three words. It really isn't a big deal — unless of course, you don't have a good answer for it.

A Question that Demands an Answer

If you're new to the industry, you probably aren't a very big fan of the Most Dreaded Question. If you've been around for a while, it probably doesn't bother you any more. Either way, one thing is certain: When the prospect asks, you're obligated to answer.

The truth is that it's a fair question. Keep in mind that you and Jack have just met. He doesn't have a clue about your opportunity. It's only natural for him to start asking questions.

A Rose by any Other Name...

The Most Dreaded Question comes in several forms. Some of the more common forms are:

- Tell me about it.
- What are you talking about?
- Whaddya' got goin' on?
- Tell me more.
- Whatcha' got?
- What would I be doing?

No matter what form the MDQ takes, the spirit of the question remains the same. This means you don't need a separate response for each variation.

Your Response

You may have a company-specific response or you may prefer to use a generic response like the ones described in this chapter. All effective responses to the Most Dreaded Question have certain characteristics in common.

Respectful

By the time that Jack asks the Most Dreaded Question, you and he have already been engaged in conversation. Naturally, you have been applying the principles of prospecting throughout, so by this point Jack likes you and he is primed to receive you offer. Don't blow it by responding in a way that may come across as flippant or facetious. Make sure your response is relevant and respectful.

Ambiguous

It's okay to empathize with Jack's curiosity, but don't reward it. You owe him an answer, but not necessarily a direct one, and certainly not a detailed one. The problem with providing detailed answers is that you run the risk of telling Jack enough for him to say "no" but not enough for him to say "yes." He ends up making his decision on the spot and your prospecting attempt is doomed. An effective answer to "What is it?" has enough content for the prospect to perceive that you answered but not enough for him to make a decision.

End with Another Question

In earlier chapters, you learned that the person asking the questions controls the conversation. If you're not careful, answering one of Jack's questions will encourage him to ask others. If this process is not checked, you'll end up handing complete control of the conversation over to Jack. The only way to regain control of the conversation after the Most Dreaded Question is to ask another question. An effective response to the MDQ involves following your answer with another question of your own.

Examples

This section provides some examples that illustrate the concepts described above. Each example picks up with you asking the magic question. Use these generic responses as models for developing your own.

Example 1

Y:	Are you open to other ways of making money as long as they don't take too much time?
P:	That depends. What exactly are you talking about?
Y:	Well, I'm part of a team that has a valuable solution to a common problem. The real question is: Are you at a point in life where you would be open to explore outside opportunities?

Notice the timing of Jack's question. He asked his version of the Most Dreaded Question immediately after you asked your magic question. You asked the first question, but rather than answer you, he asked a question of his own. This is where you will either lose control or keep control of the conversation. Let's take a closer look at your response:

Raw Phrase

Well, I'm part of a team that has a valuable solution to a common problem. The real question is: Are you at a point in life where you would be open to explore outside opportunities?

Outline

Well,[1] I'm part of a team[2] that has a valuable solution to a common problem[3]. The real question is[4]: Are you at a point in life where you would be open to explore outside opportunities?[5]

Notes

1. This is a transition phrase. It tells Jack that you're thinking about how best to answer his question. It encourages him to expect a quality answer.

2. Using the term "team" tells Jack that you are part of something much bigger than you are. This helps him to realize that he does not have enough information to form an accurate opinion of whatever "it" is.

3. This phrase tells Jack what it is that you do. You provide a "valuable solution to a common problem." It doesn't really say much, but it's enough of an answer to proceed. Additionally, the word "valuable" introduces the connotation of money. You may choose to substitute other words (e.g., "profitable" or "lucrative") depending on the level of Jack's sophistication. If you have a company-specific response, use it in place of this phrase.

4. Now that you have *answered* Jack's question, it's time to regain control. This phrase implies that Jack's question isn't even real. In effect, you are telling Jack, politely and gracefully, *your question is not relevant, but I answered it anyway.*

5. Jack never answered your magic question so ask it again, in a slightly different form. He owes you a yes/no answer. If you don't get an answer to your question, you won't know whether to hand him a prospecting tool.

At this point, you have demonstrated respect for Jack by answering his question. You have also pointed out, ever so subtlety, that he has not shown you the same respect. By repeating your question, he has an opportunity to redeem himself.

Remember, professionals sort. You don't care if he is interested or not. You just want an answer. The response outlined above, will get an answer nearly every time. Later in the chapter, you'll find an example of how to handle a prospect that refuses to follow the rules.

Example 2

Y:	Are you open to other ways of making money as long as they don't take too much time?
P:	Sure. Who isn't?
Y:	If I loaned you an interesting DVD, would you at least take a look at it over the next couple of days?
P:	Yeah, I would.
Y:	*(hand him the DVD)*
P:	What's this thing about?
Y:	It's about running your own home-based business. It's only about 16 minutes long. Do you think the next two days would give you enough time to take a look?

Notice the timing is different in this example. This time, Jack answers your magic question. He doesn't ask the Most Dreaded Question until after you have handed him a tool. This subtle shift in timing gives you an advantage.

By the time he asks, "What's this thing about?" (his version of the MDQ), he's holding your DVD. When you respond, assume he's asking about the DVD, not about the opportunity. This is an easier question to answer.

Jack is really asking about the opportunity, not the DVD, but he won't bother correcting you. By ending with another question, you regain control of the conversation. As soon as he answers, you're past the Most Dreaded Question and off to the next step.

Note: You want to have a collection of different magic questions. However, the response suggested in this scenario seems to work no matter what magic question you use.

Example 3

Y:	Are you open to other ways of making money as long as they don't take too much time?
P:	That depends. What exactly are you talking about?
Y:	Well, I'm part of a team that has a valuable solution to a common problem. The real question is: Are you at a point in life where you would be open to explore outside opportunities?
P:	I don't know. You still haven't told me what you do.

In this example, Jack is standing his ground. He is refusing to answer your question until he is satisfied with your response. Generally, this reaction indicates one of the following:

• You've done something to raise Jack's defenses
• You were unsuccessful lowering his defenses
• Jack is naturally suspicious and/or cautious. Perhaps he's a Green personality (**Chameleon of Many Colors,** Chapter 14).

The more you master the principles of prospecting, the less likely Jack is to respond in this manner. Nevertheless, some people are determined to look every gift horse in the mouth; it's just the way they are. You should prepare for this type of reaction. Try this on for size, "It's not important. It was a long shot anyway."

Afterwards, go about your business as if the conversation never occurred. Be prepared to walk away. There are other fish in the sea. Jack may feel left out and not let you drop the subject so quickly, but that's not the intent. The intent is to move on to someone who is interested. Don't be afraid to walk away. The fact is that if Jack is truly open to the notion of exploring opportunities, he won't be obstinate or wear you down with questions. Here's a rule of thumb that will serve you well: Prospects who are go-getters won't ask a lot of questions.

Assuming all goes well to this point, you're going to need a way to contact the prospect in a couple of days. The next chapter describes how to get his phone number so you can follow up.

chapter Sixteen

I've Got Your Number Now!

got number?

Here. Take my phone in case you need to call me.
—*A smart aleck from the author's past*

Once you have handed the prospect a prospecting tool, the initial conversation is nearly complete. Soon after the hand-off, each of you will be going about your business. You need to know how to contact him for the follow up. The most convenient way to follow up is by phone, so obviously, you're going to have to get his number somehow.

A Common Concern

Getting the prospect's phone number is a real sticking point for many reps. Three common reasons for this include:

1. Fear of Rejection

Perhaps you are afraid that the prospect will refuse to give you his number. After all, it would be easy for him to say something like ...

- "We just met. I'm not giving you my number."
- "What do you need my number for?"
- "I'll look at the information and if I'm interested, I'll call you."

By the end of this chapter, you will understand how to minimize the likelihood of getting a negative response.

2. You Don't Want to Infringe

Perhaps you feel as though it would be an infringement to ask for his number. Get over it. If you believe your opportunity is good for him, then you're obligated to share it. (If you don't buy into this philosophy yet, keep working, you will.)

3. You Wouldn't Give Your Own Number Out

You can change. An old Turkish proverb says, "He who builds a fence, keeps out more he keeps in." You may have missed opportunities yourself simply because you weren't more trusting of a stranger crossing your path. Here's another way to think about it: Perhaps Jack has been praying for something better to come along. He may actually be grateful that you care enough to call him back.

Requesting the Number

Getting Jack's number doesn't have to be a big deal to you or him. The bigger the deal you make out of it, the bigger a deal Jack will make out of it, so don't sweat it. The key is setting your own expectations. You should expect him to give you his number without reservation. The next couple of sections will help you to adopt the right frame of mind.

It's Only Natural

Well, if I dialed the wrong number, why did you answer?

—James Thurber

Keep in mind that you're not asking for Jack's social security number or the PIN to his bank card. You're only asking for a phone number. You won't ask for his number until after he takes possession of your prospecting tool. Jack assumes you will want the tool back, so he knows instinctively that you're going to need to call him. On a subconscious level, he expects you to ask for his number. Don't disappoint him.

It's Only Fair

When you handed Jack a DVD or magazine, you gave him something of value with no strings attached. Isn't it fair for him to give you something in return? Of course it is, and you know exactly what you're going to suggest, don't you?

Path of Least Resistance

Make up your mind that Jack is going to give you a number. Let him decide which one. By allowing him to decide which number to share, he will automatically give you the one he is most comfortable giving out. This allows Jack to stay closer to his comfort zone.

Example

As an illustration, assume the following:

- You asked your magic question
- Jack responded positively
- You hand him a DVD which he agrees to watch

The dialogue continues ...

Y:	Jack, that DVD will give you a decent overview. It's only 13 minutes and 12 seconds long. Do you think the next couple of days will give you a chance to look at it?
P:	Yeah, I think so.
Y:	Great. Here's how it works: After you check it out, you'll either want more information or you won't. If you do, we'll sit down over half a cup of coffee so we can fill in the gaps. If not, we're done. Either way, I'm OK. Does that make sense?
P:	Yeah, that makes sense.
Y:	Great. All I ask in return is a daytime number where I can touch base to see if there's any common interest. Is that fair?

Here's the phone number phrase in detail:

Raw Phrase

Great. All I ask in return is a daytime number where I can touch base to see if there's any common interest. Is that fair?

Outline

Great[1]. All I ask in return[2] is a daytime number[3] where I can touch base[4] to see if there's any common interest[5]. Is that fair?[6]

Notes

1. This is a transition phrase. It has a positive connotation (i.e., everything is fine). It also establishes the previous statement as accurate and final.

Gender Benders

Asking for a daytime number is even more important when prospecting someone of the opposite gender (especially when a man is prospecting a woman). Your intentions are honorable. Make sure your words send the proper signals.

2. This tells Jack two things: 1) you're not asking for much and 2) he owes you.

3. The term "daytime" is generic. He may give you a mobile number, a home number, or a work number. Let him give you what he's comfortable with. Notice that you asked for his *number* not his *phone number*. This is more casual and less direct. (see **Casualize and Minimize**, Chapter 13)

4. More **Casualize and Minimize**.

5. Introduces doubt, light take away (**Feeding the Birds**, Chapter 12).

6. This is another tie down. *Of course*, it's fair and you want Jack to admit it. Additionally, asking a question leaves you in control.

Night and Day

 A daytime number is well and good as long as your schedule permits you to make follow up calls during the day. If your job doesn't have enough flexibility for you to make calls during the day, you'll need to ask for an evening number instead.

Getting an evening number is essentially the same as getting a daytime number, with one exception. When you ask for an evening number, tell Jack why a daytime number won't work. You don't want to make a major production out of it, so casually mention it indirectly.

(First part of dialogue is the same as in previous example.)	
P:	Yeah, that makes sense.
Y:	Great. All I ask in return is a ~~daytime~~ number where I can touch base to see if there's any common interest. Is that fair?
P:	Sure.
Y:	Just so you know, my days are pretty crazy and I don't normally have a chance to make a lot of calls during the day. So, it probably makes sense to jot down an evening number. Make sense?

There are two differences between this example and the previous one. The first difference is omitting the word "daytime" (denoted by ~~daytime~~). The second difference is the addition of the last phrase. Notice that your explanation focuses on why an A.M. number won't work, not why you need his P.M. number. In effect, you are stating a problem and inviting him to solve it. You are appealing to his natural instinct of helping others.

Recording the number

Once Jack agrees to share his number, you'll be coasting downhill. All that remains is the act of recording his contact information.

Let Jack do the Writing

It's best to have Jack do the writing. Doing so is simple when you know that Jack has easy access to pen and paper. Typically, this will include people working in service industries (e.g., waiters, A/C technicians, bank tellers). Keep in mind Jack has already agreed that it makes sense for you to have his number, so simply say something like:

- "Make sure I have your contact info before I leave."
- "Why don't you jot down your contact info real quick?"
- "Do you have a pen handy?"

Eventually, you'll experience a situation where you hand the prospect a tool before you even know his name. The prospect knows instinctively that you don't know his name. By asking for contact info instead of a number, he will supply his name as well as the number.

Less Chance for Error

You may be a bit nervous, making you more likely to commit an error. If you do the writing, you run the risk of misunderstanding him and recording the wrong number. Perhaps, you hear him correctly, but transpose some digits as you write. Either way, you end up with the wrong number. By having Jack write his own contact information, you alleviate the risk of simple mistakes. Make sure you can read his writing before you walk away.

Jack's Full Name

When Jack first states his name, he may only share his first name. When you have him write his own contact information, you are creating another opportunity to obtain his full name. Ending up with Jack's full name is a bonus, but it isn't mandatory. In fact, in many cases, you won't even use it.

Jack Becomes a Willing Participant

Another advantage of having the prospect write his own information is that it makes him part of the process. You didn't threaten, coerce, or bribe him for it. He gave it to you of his own free will. This is significant because it completes the give-and-take cycle you established as the pattern of your conversation.

If You do the Writing

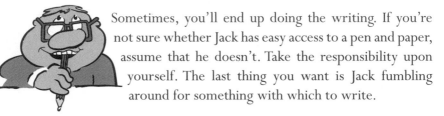

Sometimes, you'll end up doing the writing. If you're not sure whether Jack has easy access to a pen and paper, assume that he doesn't. Take the responsibility upon yourself. The last thing you want is Jack fumbling around for something with which to write.

Be casual and spontaneous about writing materials. If you come across too prepared, you look practiced. You may have orchestrated the entire encounter but you don't have to broadcast the fact. Ideally, through casual observation you've already identified what you'll be writing on. Here are some common ones that project spontaneity:

- Napkin
- Paper towel near a gas pump
- Register receipt
- Dollar bill
- Back of a business card (yours or someone else's)

Grab whatever you've chosen to write on, get your pen poised to write, and say, "Here, I'll just write on this real quick. What's the best way to get hold of you?"

If All Else Fails

If neither of you has paper and pen handy, use your phone instead. Say, "You caught me off guard." (Ha! He caught you? This subtle role reversal is both fun and effective.) "Here, just call out your number and I'll capture it in my phone. What's the correct spelling of your name?" Be sure to have Jack verify that you entered his information correctly.

When Jack Won't Play

The strategies outlined in this chapter work and they work well. With practice, they work 99.9% of the time. What about the other .1%? They're out there, so you might as well know how to deal with them.

The number one thing to keep in mind is this: you don't need Jack. You're not obligated to convince him of anything *(8ᵗʰ Law of Prospecting)*. If he is reluctant to share his phone number, then you don't want it.

If you follow the outline above, by the time he refuses to give you his number, he is already holding the prospecting tool. If he won't share his number, then have enough gumption to take your tool back. In my opinion, if Jack takes a tool from your hand, and then refuses to provide a number, he's being somewhat of a jerk. That doesn't mean you have to be a jerk in return.

Here's how to respond: Casually and lightly grasp the tool, but don't actually take it from him. As your hand begins to move toward the disc, say this: "I apologize. I thought you said you were open to explore other opportunities. I guess I misunderstood." Notice how you take responsibility for the misunderstanding. When you offer to accept the blame for his negative attitude, Jack will be completely disarmed. This response will keep your confidence intact both during and after the encounter.

JACK
867-5309

Congratulations. You now know how to get the prospect's phone number. The best part is that you didn't have to pry it from his cold, dead fingers. In the next chapter, you'll learn how to put his number to use.

chapter Seventeen

Follow Up or Fall Down

If the Phone Doesn't Ring, It's Me.
—*Jimmy Buffet song,* Last Mango in Paris *album*

When a prospect accepts your tool, examines it, and wants to know more, then it makes sense to begin sponsoring him, right? Whoa. Slow down, Turbo. Didn't you leave something out? How did you find out that he wants to know more? You followed up, that's how.

- If you don't follow up, you won't know if Jack is interested.
- If you don't know he's interested, you won't sponsor him.
- If you don't sponsor, you won't make money.

Thus, your fortune is in the follow up. Either follow up or fall down.

In the Beginning

In the beginning, you think of follow ups as distasteful, but necessary. As a result, you probably haven't given much thought how to go about it. In short, your follow ups lack structure. The times that you do call a prospect back, you're not sure what to say. As soon as Jack asks a question, you lose control of the conversation. Thus, more often than not, you talk the prospect right out of any interest he might have had.

In the beginning, you think of follow up as a separate step. Logically, it fits right between prospecting and sponsoring. Prospect (hand him a tool), follow up (check to see if he wants to find out more), and if he does, begin to sponsor him. This approach is perfectly logical. It is also fatally flawed.

Let There Be Light

Let's shed a little light on the subject of follow up.

Jack's opinion of you is a major factor in determining how much interest he will have in your opportunity. He begins to form his almighty opinion the moment you meet. Everything you do and say from the very beginning contributes to Jack's opinion of you and your opportunity. Thus, the follow -up process begins at the very start of the encounter. If you wait and start the follow up after the first encounter, you're starting with a disadvantage.

If I Want Your Opinion, I'll Give It To You

> *Opinion is ultimately determined by the feelings and not by the intellect.*
>
> —Herbert Spencer

I once read that diplomacy is the art of letting someone else have your way. Similarly, you can think of prospecting as the art of forming someone else's opinion. By employing the principles of prospecting, you make a positive impact on Jack's almighty opinion. The following table summarizes how the principles mold the prospect's opinion of you and your opportunity:

The Principle of ...	Affects Prospect's Opinion by ...
100% Chance of Sunshine	Paying him compliments
Curiosity Paid the Cat	Showing genuine interest in him
Mental Judo	Building rapport
You Let the Dogs Out	Demonstrating your respect for him
Feeding the Birds	Enhancing your sincerity
Casualize & Minimize	Making you more relatable

When you purposefully shape the prospect's opinion during the first encounter, you make the follow up call simpler and more effective.

Dr. Jekyll and Mr. Phone

I know all too well about struggling with follow through. It's one thing to hand out a DVD or a magazine. It's an entirely different matter to call the person afterward. I would go to make a follow up call only to find that my phone had gone through a horrifying transformation. It had once been a normal looking, inanimate object sitting on the desk. What I found in its place was a breathing 500-pound monster with blotches of hair and a bad overbite. It was frightening and I didn't want to go anywhere near it.

Okay, maybe I'm exaggerating — maybe — but only a wee little bit. The fact is I was terrified of calling prospects to follow up. I desperately needed a way to force myself to make follow up calls. I found a solution. It involved tricking myself. I didn't know it then, but the solution had additional benefits I never anticipated.

Integrity Trumps Fear

My plan was simple. I would put my integrity on the line. I knew that if I told the prospect I would be calling that I would have no choice but to honor my word. For me, honoring my word was more compelling than the fear of following up. If you are the same way, follow the pattern described below, and you'll be making all of your follow up calls too.

Let's say you're prospecting Jack and have successfully accomplished the following steps:

- You asked the magic question
- Jack expressed an interest
- You gave him a tool which he is currently holding
- He agrees to check it out over the next two days
- You ask for and obtain his phone number

Now say something like this:

Jack, the next couple of days are going to be kind of crazy. I'm not exactly sure when I will be calling but you have my word that I will call within the next day or two. Is that alright?

Is there any doubt that this phrase puts your integrity on the line? The day I started using this line, is the day I stopped procrastinating on follow up calls.

Making the Follow up Call

This strategy makes the follow up call a breeze. To illustrate, assume that you dial Jack's number so you can follow up on a DVD you gave him two days ago. His phone is ringing now...

P:	Hello?
Y:	Is this Jack?
P:	Yeah, this is Jack.
Y:	Jack, this is Russ. You may not remember me, but we bumped into each other a couple of days ago and I loaned you some information. (pause)
P:	Yeah, I remember.
Y:	Do you have a quick moment?
P:	Yes, I've a got a minute or two.
Y:	Well, I told you I would be calling and I'm just making good on my word.
P:	Okay.

Both the content and order of your lines are important to a smooth start. Let's look at the dynamics of this dialogue:

1st Line: "Is this Jack?"

Make sure that you're talking to the right person. You don't want to jump into a follow up conversation with the wrong person. If would be a truly awkward moment if you started blabbing about an outside opportunity to a person who turned out to be Jack's boss.

Sometimes I use first name, sometimes last name. It depends on my perception of the prospect and his culture. In my experience, white cultures tend to respond well to a more casual form of address so I use first name with them. Other cultures seem to enjoy the respect of a more formal address such as Mr. or Mrs. Using both first and last name is too formal for my own preference so I rarely use them together.

2nd Line: "Jack, this is Russ..."

Raw Phrase

Jack, this is Russ. You may not remember me, but we bumped into each other a couple of days ago and I loaned you some information.

Outline

Jack, this is Russ[1]. You may not remember me[2], but we[3] bumped[4] into each other a couple[5] of days ago and I loaned[6] you some information[7]. (pause)[8]

Notes

1. Refer to yourself using first name only. You want Jack to think of you as a friend. You don't use your last name addressing friends so don't use it here.

2. Of course, Jack remembers you, but this phrase is unassuming. It demonstrates humility.

3. The plural pronoun, "we", makes Jack partly responsible for your encounter. (Isn't that rich?)

4. "Bumped into" is a casual term (Chapter 13, *Casualize & Minimize*). It makes the original encounter seem more like an isolated event, not intentionally orchestrated by a professional prospector.

5. Another imprecise, casual term

6. As far as Jack knows, the tool he's holding is only on loan. If your tools are inexpensive, you may never intend to get it back but there's no need for Jack to know so at this point.

7. Information is an ambiguous term having two advantages: 1) you won't have to remember what type of tool you gave him (DVD, magazine, etc.) and 2) it provides an alternative to the word opportunity. You may have to call more than once before he looks at the tool. Don't overdo the word opportunity. It can get old fast.

8. The pause gives Jack a chance to say, "Yeah, I remember".

3rd Line: "Do you have a quick moment?"

Always, always, always clear the call. You have no idea what Jack is in the middle of when you call. Jack trusted you with his number. Don't betray his trust by rudely interrupting him. As soon as Jack realizes who you are, clear the call. Ask whether it's a good time for him to talk.

Here are several phrases that clear the call:

"Did I catch you at a good time?"

This question does show respect by clearing the call, but who isn't always in the middle of something? If Jack responds by saying something like, "Man, what a crazy day," you won't know if you're intruding or not. This phrase is better than not clearing the call at all, but it doesn't qualify very well.

"May I have a moment of your time?"

This question simultaneously projects professionalism and confidence. Moreover, it is extraordinarily difficult to say no to. Save it for following up with prospects that are more sophisticated. This phrase will make you stand out in the crowd. One time, I used it to clear the call with an insurance executive. His response was, "Well Russ, I appreciate you asking, but I'm in a meeting right now. Can you call me later?" It was easy to call him back and he gladly accepted my call.

"Did I catch you at a bad time?"

For years, this was my favorite. It shows respect and gets right to the point. The word "bad" is a strong qualifier. It forces Jack to evaluate the priority of his immediate activity. Only truly high priority tasks will rank higher than your call. The prospect will normally say something like "No, I've got a minute."

Do you have a quick moment?"

This is my current favorite. It shows plenty of respect, it projects a casual speech pattern, and it tells Jack that you're not going to take much of his time. Jack perceives your call as respectful, congenial, and unobtrusive. It will nearly always cause the prospect to give you some time.

4th Line: "Well, I told you I would be calling..."

"Well, I told you I would be calling and I'm just making good on my word." Read it again. Does it say that you tell Jack that you're calling to do a follow up? Does it say that you're calling to convince him to join your opportunity? No. It says that you are merely calling because you promised you would.

Serendipities Abound

Earlier in this chapter, I mentioned discovering benefits to this approach that I had not initially anticipated. The first unexpected benefit is the fact that it completely disarms the prospect. Jack might be expecting you to start a full-tilt recruiting pitch. He finds it refreshing when you don't. Thus, he is more relaxed, more open-minded, and more likely to take the next step.

The second benefit is less tangible but just as powerful. By honoring your word, you are demonstrating integrity. Remember, you and Jack have no history as of yet. You start out with zero credibility. Making good on your word begins to establish credibility with your new acquaintance. It is a way of establishing a track record of reliability, vital to team building.

Not Now, I Have a Headache

When you clear the call, you are asking Jack whether it's a good time for him to speak with you. Clearing the call means asking a yes or no question. You hope he has time to talk, but he may not. When Jack tells you it's not a good time to talk, be professional and back off. Don't over-stay your welcome. As you end the conversation, encourage Jack to suggest an alternative time for you to call back. If he does offer an alternative, he is buying in to your next call. This is huge because as long as you're calling at his suggestion, he can't very well consider you a bother.

Exactly how you back off depends on Jack's manner. Learn to read the situation by listening to his words, his tone, and his pace. The number of ways Jack can respond is infinite. The examples below represent a cross section of common responses. Each example includes specific things for you to say in return. These are merely suggestions; things that work for me. Use them as models for designing your own responses.

"Actually Russ, this really isn't a good time. Can we talk some other time?"

Analysis: Notice here that Jack's response is short and to the point. He offers no explanation. He is probably in a hurry. His suggestion of some other time is vague and implies that he is not in a hurry to continue the conversation.

Response: If he's in a hurry to get off the phone, then you should sound like you're in a hurry to let him go. Try this: "No problem, Jack. Do I have permission to touch base next week?

"This is a bad week. Can you call me next week sometime?"

Analysis: This response tells you there's something unique about the current week. When Jack is specific about the duration of the "bad" time, he is hinting about when to call back. In this example, he is going so far as to suggest a time for you to call back.

Response: You still have time to squeeze in another question. Ask him to be more specific: "Absolutely. Is there one day that would be better or worse than the others?" This may sound odd as you read it, but Jack will know exactly what you're asking and he will give you a quality response.

"I'm in the middle of something right now, but I do want to talk to you. Can you call me later?"

Analysis: This is a positive response. You know there's genuine interest, you just caught him at an inopportune time. While "later" isn't specific, the overall tone implies that he would like to talk soon.

Response: Assume that he means later the same day: "You mean later today?" If he says, "Yes," ask, "What time would you suggest?" If he says, "No," then he will suggest another day in which case you ask, "In general, are mornings or afternoons better for you?"

"I'm just about to step out. I'll call you later."

Analysis: This is the response of a person with a busy schedule. It's hard to tell from this statement whether he has a genuine interest or if he's dismissing you indefinitely. Don't count on him calling. If you don't take control, he'll leave you in the dark.

Response: I prefer to have a better idea of where I stand with the Jackster. The idea is to pin him down to a more specific answer. Here's one way to do it: "No problem. Do you mean later today?" At this point, he will say "yes" or he will name another day. As soon as he answers, say, "Well Jack, I know you have a thousand things going on, so if I don't hear from you by then, do I have permission to call you back?" It is nearly impossible for him to tell you no. As soon as he gives you permission, the monkey is on his back and he's the one who put it there. In essence, if you have to call back, it's because he did not honor his word. You politely, professionally, and purposefully nailed him down and you did it with his permission.

Your Integrity Is Still On The Line

Don't forget the basic premise behind your follow up. You are just making good on your word. When you agree to call Jack on a specific day or at a specific time, you are giving him your word all over again. It is imperative that you continue to honor the agreement. At times, this can be a real pain but the payoff is worth it.

Try This

Sometimes it's fun to throw out one final question just to leave a lasting impression. It's one of my favorite questions of all. This question is guaranteed to make you stand out in the crowd. It exudes professionalism, and confidence. It demonstrates sophistication and experience. In the south, you could call it a "real humdinger." Here's how it works:

It's January and you call Jack to follow up. He tells you that he's tied up for the next month. After a brief dialogue, he suggests that the middle of February would be a good time for you to check back. Now say this, "That sounds great, Jack. You won't get offended if you don't hear from me before February 15th, will you?" Jack has no choice but to be impressed.

The Time is Right!

Up to this point, the chapter has focused on what to say when you first call, and how to handle scenarios where you catch Jack when he can't stop to talk. Eventually, you will catch him at a good time. What do you do then?

Authors' Notes: Your success team (aka upline) may have an outline already. If so, use it. If the suggestions contradict your team philosophy, stick with your team outline.

Here's an outline:

- Let him know you won't take much of his time
- Encourage him to say something positive about the prospecting tool
- Move him to the next step (e.g., sit-down presentation)

Example

Y:	Do you have a quick moment?
P:	Yes, I've a got a minute or two.
Y:	Well, I told you I would be calling and I'm just making good on my word.
P:	Okay.
Y:	I didn't call to monopolize your time, but I did want to call and find out what you liked best about the information. [1]
P:	Well, the product looks pretty good. [2]
Y:	Yeah, that's what I said too. What do you say we sit down over a half cup of coffee and fill in the gaps? [3]
P:	We can do that.
Y:	Would you prefer something right before or right after work? [4]
P:	Mornings are more predictable.
Y:	You know, there's a coffee shop across the street from where we met. Would that work for you? [5]
P:	Sure
Y:	What day later this week would work for you? [6]
P:	Friday would be okay.
Y:	Would seven o'clock that morning be okay? [7]
P:	Yeah.
Y:	Great. Do you have pen handy? [8]
P:	Yeah.
Y:	I'll leave you my number in case something unexpected pops up. Alright? [9]
P:	Good idea.

Y:	*(Call out your number slowly and clearly)* Okay Jack, if I don't hear different, I'll see you Friday morning at 7 a.m. there at the coffee shop by your office. Sound good? [10]
P:	See you then.
Y:	One more thing Jack: there's something about me you should know. You would have no way of knowing otherwise, so I'm going share it. (pause) I'm *always* where I say I'm going to be when I say I'm going to be there. The down side of being so punctual is that I tend to expect it of everyone else. That won't be an issue in your case will it? [11]
P:	No. I'll be there.
Y:	Great. I look forward to our visit. I really appreciate your time Jack. Have a great day. [12]
P:	You too. (Wait for him to hang up first.) [13]

Notes

1. This phrase accomplishes three goals: 1) sets him at ease by telling him you won't take much of his time, 2) encourages him to say something positive about the information you gave him, and 3) if he answers positively, it will give you insight as to his primary interest. Also, don't ask what he thinks. He doesn't know enough to have an educated opinion so don't ask for one.

2. It doesn't matter what he likes best.

3. Agree with whatever he identifies as his favorite part. Notice the use of *Casualize and Minimize* (Chapter 13). If your team does something other than a sit-down suggest that instead.

4. "A-B close" — give him two choices either one of which will work for you.

5. In *Curiosity Paid the Cat*, you found out where he works. Now, knowing the location makes it easy to suggest a convenient place to meet.

6. Another "A-B close." Notice how you suggest something this week. He may not share your sense of urgency but there's no harm in trying.

7. Make a specific suggestion or you may be waiting all day for him to decide.

8. Don't say. "Get a pen so I can give you my number." Ask a question instead.

9. You don't need his permission, but questions work *so* very well.

10. Repeat the specifics to alleviate confusion (yours and his).

11. This is huge! This one statement can virtually eliminate no-shows. Speak it clearly and with total conviction. If Jack is used to scheduling appointments as a normal part of his occupation (e.g., CPA, insurance agent), do NOT use this statement otherwise you may insult him. When you do use it, say it with a big smile on your face. That will make sure you don't come across as condescending.

12. Show some manners. Make his time sound more valuable than yours. Make sure you sound sincere. Put a slight emphasis on "great."

13. Don't let him hear you hang up. You don't want him to get the impression that he's just another notch on your belt.

Congratulations. You've moved Jack to the next step.

When Jack Won't Look at the Information

 Have you noticed how some people never seem to get around to looking at the prospecting tool? You call Jack several times and every time he claims to be interested, but he still hasn't looked at the information you loaned him. This is a common source of frustration for many reps (especially ones new to our industry). This section discusses how to shorten your ride on the no-I-haven't-watched-the-DVD merry-go-round.

The Nature of the Ride

Before you try to stop the merry-go-round, understand it. Look at it from the perspective of the prospect. Pretend you're Jack:

- At lunch, a friendly stranger offers you a chance to check out an opportunity.
- You express genuine interest and agree to look at a DVD.
- When you get back to the office, your manager grills your department on a missed deadline. You work late to compensate.
- When you get home, the kids need help with homework.

- Once the kids are in bed, you finally have time to watch the DVD, but will you? You're tired and all you really want to do is watch some TV. You can always watch the DVD tomorrow.

- The cycle repeats...

You see, Jack's train of life is already racing down the track. You're jumping up and down on the platform as it goes by yelling, "Hey, what about me? Slow down!" Understanding these dynamics from Jack's viewpoint can minimize your own frustration. Jack's not trying to frustrate you or waste your time. All you have to do is make it so easy for Jack to watch the DVD, that he feels compelled to do so. There are several strategies at your disposal. As you study them, keep in mind that it's not necessary to use all of these strategies simultaneously. With practice, you will learn to discern their appropriate application.

Author's Note: Some companies make both magazines and DVD's available to their reps. In my experience, magazines are more likely to be used by the prospect than DVDs simply because the media is easier to browse through. Since prospect procrastination is more of an issue with DVD's, this section focuses on that media. Even so, most of the concepts translate to the use of magazines as well.

Be Enthusiastic

The more enthusiastic you are when you hand Jack the DVD, the more interest he will have in watching it. If your energy level is low, you'll be no different from Jack later that night when he's in front of the TV. Jack has to sense something different about you. He needs to smell hope. He needs to know that you're taking life by the tail. In short, he needs to know that you have something he doesn't.

You accomplish this through your tone and your attitude. Don't use direct language to tell him these things. Don't be condescending. Be upbeat. Be personable. Portray a quiet confidence while being humble. Demonstrate a controlled enthusiasm about the information on your DVD. Read that again. Your enthusiasm is about the information on the DVD, not about the fact that Jack agreed to watch it. This subtle difference is critical. If Jack gets the feeling that you're thinking, "Whoo-hoo! I got one!"— you're wasting your time (and his).

Convey a Sense of Urgency

This can be a tricky one. Put an emphasis on getting the DVD back. The goal here is to find a balance between being in a hurry and not pressuring the prospect.

Set His Expectations

If Jack believes that the DVD is a long-winded sales pitch, he is more likely to procrastinate. Help him to understand that the video is short and interesting. Do this after he has agreed to watch and after he has given you his number. I typically say something like this:

Just so you know—that video is only 16 minutes and 43 seconds long so you won't have to plan a whole evening around it. In fact, you won't even have time to pop popcorn. *grin*

Tell Jack precisely how much time it will take. Many prospecting DVD's are right at fifteen minutes long. Don't tell Jack it's about 15 minutes long. Fifteen minutes is a period of time used so commonly in everyday conversation, that we tend to use it haphazardly. To some people 15 minutes is anything less than 30 minutes. When you use a precise time, Jack will know that you're not exaggerating. He will be more inclined to watch if he knows exactly how long it is.

Another way to set his expectation is by letting him know that he will find the video interesting. Remember, you know what's on the DVD, Jack doesn't. He may be expecting a fast-talking, in-your-face, high-pressure sales pitch. Set his mind at ease. Say something like this:

If you're like most people, you're going to be pleasantly surprised by how much you enjoy that video.

Integrity Trumps Procrastination

No matter how expert you are at prospecting, some prospects are going to procrastinate. You call once, twice, three times, and get the same response every time: "I really want to watch it. I just haven't had time." Of course, Jack *had* the time; he just didn't *take* the time.

Maybe he isn't truly interested. Perhaps he's a Yellow personality and is concerned about offending you. Do you want to keep calling someone who isn't genuinely interested? I hope not. Even if he does have genuine interest, if you keep calling, you appear desperate. Bad idea. One strategy in particular can break this cycle for some prospects.

Let's say you've gotten Jack on the phone twice to follow up, but both times, he told you he hasn't had time to watch the DVD. You've had enough. Try the following dialogue:

P:	Russ, I'm sorry I just haven't had the time to get to it.
Y:	Jack, there's no need to apologize. I know what's on the disc. (smiling as you say it) Is it okay if I ask you a question?[1]
P:	Sure.
Y:	Well, I'm just wondering if you have any real interest or if you're just being polite.[2]
P:	No, I really am interested.
Y:	Okay. So tell me this: how much longer do you need to watch it? And remember, it's only a few minutes long.[3]
P:	I can watch it by Friday.
Y:	You know Jack, I realize that we barely know each other, but my initial impression of you is that you are a man of your word. Is that correct?[4]
P:	Absolutely
Y:	Great. Then when I touch base on Friday, you would have watched the DVD?[5]
P:	Yes.
Y:	Okay. I'll buzz you on Friday.[6]
P:	Okay.
Y:	Have a great day.[7]

Notes

1. Disarm Jack by telling him there's no need to apologize. The next line ("I know…") introduces a bit of levity (make sure you are smiling). By now, you know that ending with a question leaves you in control and secures his buy-in.

2. This line gives Jack a way out. If he has no interest, let him go. It's not actually a question, but if you follow the script, he will answer it as if it is.

3. This question allows Jack to specify the time frame. He may not share your sense of urgency, but it's critical that you let him specify the time. At this point in the conversation, you also remind him that watching the DVD won't require a large investment of his time.

4. This line is a setup. You're about to find out what he's made of. I've never had any one admit that they're not a person of integrity. (If he answers no to this question, get off the phone!) He's going to know that he walked into a corner. If you stick with the script, he won't be offended. Otherwise, be careful.

5. You're asking a yes or no question, but in reality, there's only one way for him to respond—in the affirmative.

6. You just whacked him with a velvet hammer. It's time to be nice and casual.

7. Sign off with an upbeat, genuine tone.

This script is strong medicine. It can really stop the merry-go-round of wasted time, but be aware that it takes finesse and confidence to pull it off.

You just walked Jack through the process of putting his integrity on the line. Don't ruin your own integrity by forgetting to call on the appointed day. When you do call, you'll have a much better idea of where he stands with respect to your offer.

Know When to Fold 'Em

You're going to encounter some prospects that no matter what you do or say, never watch the DVD. You're going to wonder why they ever took the DVD to begin with. Who knows? As Jim Rohn says, "Don't sign up for that class." Just know that it's part of the process. When you realize that you're dealing with a professional time waster, cut him loose.

Here's a good way to do it:

Jack, I'm getting a sense that this just isn't the best time for you to consider an outside opportunity. I'd like to encourage you to keep the DVD for future reference. That way if something changes, you'll have my contact information handy. I'd be honored to have you on the team, but it has to be the right timing in your life. Don't you agree?

This script will edify Jack and leave him with a positive attitude toward you and your opportunity. This is different application of **You Let the Dogs Out** (Chapter 11). You never know — one day he may call you back.

> *Ninety-five percent of everything you do in network marketing is a complete, utter waste of time. The other five percent will make you wealthy. The catch is that while you're doing it, you won't know which is which.*
>
> **—K. S.**

chapter Eighteen

Putting It All Together

A good puzzle, it's a fair thing. Nobody is lying. It's very clear, and the problem depends just on you.

— *Erno Rubik*

A Real World Example

You may be thinking, "Okay, Russ, as I read about the principles, they make total sense. I see the wisdom of your words and I understand how to activate individual principles by following the scripts. However, I'm still not entirely sure how to put all this information together."

Relax, that's exactly what this chapter covers. You're about to see an entire prospecting encounter from beginning to end. This example is an actual account of a specific personal experience.

A prospecting encounter is much like a play. There is a stage where the encounter unfolds. There is a setting, which determines the mood and overall tone of the encounter. Finally, there is a script, which contains the actual words that make up the conversation.

1. Stage

It is spring, the sun is shining, and the weather is warm[1]. As I'm driving, I see a man dressed in a suit getting out of his car[2] parked at a gas pump[3]. The gas pump is on my side of the road[4]. The opposite side of the same pump is unoccupied[5]. My own fuel gauge shows my tank is half full[6]. The time is 2:30 in the afternoon[7].

Notes

1. Nice weather is important because I realize that this encounter will unfold outside and I don't want to compete with bad weather. Who wants to stand in the rain or cold to talk to strangers? The prospect surely doesn't.

2. This leads me to assume that the prospect just arrived. This is important because it means that I will likely have enough time to prospect him.

3. I assume that he will remain outside while he fills his tank.

4. It would take too much time to cross to the other side of the road.

5. That's exactly where I want to be—close enough to start a conversation.

6. I don't need gas, but I do need a plausible reason to pull in next to the prospect.

7. He must have some control over his schedule.

2. Setting

*Authors note: The setting is ascertained by making rapid observations and then translating these observations into assumptions, based on stereotypes (see **Chameleon of Many Colors,** Chapter 14). Doing so is not an exact science. Always be prepared to correct mistakes made in this phase.*

I had already observed that the prospect is wearing a suit[1]. As I park my own car, I make additional observations. His shirt is light blue in color[2]. He is driving a late model Mercedes.[3] The car isn't a convertible.[4] He does not appear to be in a particular hurry,[5] but he definitely moves with purpose and confidence.[6] The car has no other occupants (people or pets).[7] His facial expression is neutral[8].

Notes

1. I assume that he's an executive. Which indicates that he is: 1) success-oriented, 2) a go-getter by nature, and 3) has better than average communication skills. Based on the time of day, he's either the "guy in charge" or he's self-employed (perhaps a highly compensated consultant).

2. If his shirt was brightly colored, (particularly an unorthodox color), I would assume him to have a blue★ personality. A light blue shirt by itself isn't enough for me to assume red!, yellow±, or green?, but in the absence of a bright colored one, I am inclined to rule out the blue personality.

3. Red personalities like powerful, expensive automobiles.

4. Weak, circumstantial evidence in the case against a blue personality

5. If he's running late to his next appointment, he may be less inclined to stop for a chat. Not being on someone else's schedule is further evidence that he's used to being in control.

6. These are common red traits.

7. There is less chance of distraction if he's alone.

8. If he's worried, depressed, or in deep thought, I may be an unwelcome distraction. If I see a negative expression, I may or may not approach him. If his expression is neutral or positive, it's a definite "go."

Given these clues, I assume that he's an executive with a red personality who has the time and inclination to chat. Remember, I could be wrong on any or all accounts. This is merely a starting point.

3. Script

The first thing I do is get the fuel flowing into my own tank. I lock the pump on the slowest possible setting (my tank isn't empty and I want to postpone the pump clicking off for as long as possible). As I do this, I'm taking inventory of what I know about relating to Red personalities: Be direct. Don't be too funny, and speak confidently. I check the status of my own facial expression and crank up my positive attitude. My final preparation is that of visualizing him enthusiastically accepting a prospecting tool.

Upon getting the pump started, I looked at the prospect. I was hoping for immediate eye contact. It didn't happen. What follows is the conversation I had with the suspect, I mean, prospect.

Russ: How's it goin'?

> *Principle: Put a Funnel in his Ear*
> *Funnel: Opening line*
> *Other Chapter(s): Making Contact*
> *Comments: standard opening; Since we weren't making eye contact, I said this without looking at him. I made sure to say it in a way that he would realize that I was speaking to him.*

Jack: So far, so good.

> *Comments: a common response; At this point, it is natural for the prospect to look at you and he did. The content of this phrase is neutral. Tone of voice and facial expression can provide strong clues as to how open the prospect is to further conversation. In this encounter, even his tone was neutral. Since he didn't respond negatively, I resorted to my default action — press on.*

Russ: You sound like you're expecting trouble.

> *Funnel: Opening line*
> *Principle: Put a Funnel in his Ear, 100% Chance of Sunshine*
> *Other Chapter(s): Making Contact*
> *Comments: My standard response to "So far, so good." I grin slightly as I say it. This gives him a clue that Russ is making an attempt at humor.*

Jack: (chuckle) No, not really.

> *Comments: A chuckle is always a good sign. When you get a chuckle as part of*

the opening line, go for it. It's time to enter the main conversation.

Russ: Work around here?

> *Funnel: Main conversation*
>
> *Principle: Curiosity Paid the Cat*
>
> *Comments: The first question as outlined in Curiosity Paid the Cat; This question started the main conversation. (Remember, the further you get into the funnel, the more similar your conversations will be.)*
>
> *As he began to chuckle, I began to smile (Chameleon of Many Colors). Anytime you can start the questions while the prospect is smiling, do it.*
>
> *I observed his reaction to my question. Did he seem to raise his guard? He did not. I knew that so far, he was relaxed and comfortable. Reds are confident by nature. Additionally, I had taken care to keep my tone light. Considering these factors, I concluded that the remainder of the conversation would go smoothly. It would merely be a matter of going through the motions.*

Jack: No, I work downtown.

> *Comments: It really didn't matter what he said here (as long as he wasn't negative). I was still getting the conversation started.*

Russ: You're a better man than me. I don't have the patience to drive in that kind of traffic everyday. What do you do professionally?

> *Funnel: Main conversation*
>
> *Principle: 100% Chance of Sunshine, Curiosity Paid the Cat*
>
> *Comments: In this situation, I saw a way to tailor my response to his previous answer. I knew the drive downtown is horrific and I incorporated this knowledge into my response. This is a good way to transition to the next question, but it isn't necessary.*
>
> *Notice that the first sentence of this phrase was a compliment. The next sentence explains the compliment. I postponed the second question until the end of the phrase. I could have gone straight to asking about his profession, but I saw an opening to compliment him so I took it.*

Jack: I'm in advertising.

> *Principle: Chameleon of Many Colors*
>
> *Comments: He had no choice but to answer. I was being too nice for him to*

not cooperate. He did so with no hesitation and no indication of cautiousness. If I had seen such a clue, I would have re-evaluated my assumption of his personality. Specifically, I might have suspected Green instead of Red. (As a result, I would have made three key mental notes: 1) avoid other attempts at humor, 2) move slowly if and when I decide to step in for a handshake, and 3) be overtly nonchalant when I ask my magic question).

At the time, I did not know anyone else associated with advertising, so I didn't have a direct or indirect connection to mention (Curiosity Paid the Cat).

Russ: Are you the one that comes up with all those hilarious Bud Light commercials?

Funnel: Main conversation

Principle: 100% Chance of Sunshine

Comments: Ordinarily, at this point, I would ask the "really" question (Curiosity Paid the Cat). Instead, I saw an opportunity to ask something specific to his response. With practice, you'll begin to identify situation-specific customizations as well.

This is another compliment. Even non-drinkers like me enjoy the Bud commercials. Of course, I didn't really believe he was the one who came up with them, but the mere suggestion was a compliment nonetheless.

Additionally, the commercials in question are humorous. This allowed me to inject some more humor without being the source of the humor (just in case he is a Green).

Jack: Not exactly. (smiling)

Comments: It really didn't matter what he said here. The important thing is that he answered. Remember the pattern — I asked, he answered. (lull in the conversation)

I wasn't sure how much longer it would be before the prospect finished with his gas. If I asked my magic question at this point, he may have too much time to start asking me questions. Thus, I decided, that instead of continuing the conversation flow, I would drop the conversation and use the "Columbo" approach (Mental Judo). This is where many reps go wrong: it's not necessary to have a continuous dialogue until you get around to the subject of opportunity. Sometimes it's best to let the conversation fade off until the encounter is about to end. This was one of those times.

Eventually, his pump clicked off. This was the prospecting moment. I waited until he was just about to open his door and then I said ...

Russ: By the way, I know this is coming out of left field, but it is okay if I ask you a question?

Funnel: Prospecting moment

Principle: Mental Judo

Comments: This is straight out of the chapter on Mental Judo. By this point, he had chuckled at least twice and there had been a lull in the lull in conversation. His guard was down.

Jack: Sure.

Comments: I waited for his response (I asked, he answered). He responded affirmatively giving me permission to proceed with the next question.

Russ: Do you ever look at outside opportunities if they don't conflict with your current interests?

Funnel: Magic Question

Principle: Chameleon of Many Colors

Other Chapter(s): Magic Questions

Comments: Executives know that opportunities equate to money. Similarly, I assumed that he understood time management — if there was something he had interest in, he found a way to make the time (this is especially true of Red personalities). For these reasons, I didn't use the words "money" or "time." This is how I tailored the magic question to the prospect.

Jack: Sure. What do you have in mind?

Comments: Notice how the first part of his response, "sure," was an affirmative answer. Then he asked me a question (Most Dreaded Question). This was the moment or truth, if I wasn't careful, I would lose control of the conversation. The only way to retain control was to counter with another question of my own. Here's how I responded ...

Russ: Well, this isn't exactly the ideal setting for a worthwhile conversation. If I loaned you some information, would you at least take a look?

See: The Most Dreaded Question

Comments: This response side-stepped his question completely. Rather than give him a direct answer, I pointed out that it would be silly to discuss it on the driveway of a convenience store. Note: My choice of words did not ridicule him or his idea in any way. This logic worked well because executives conduct business in offices or over meals but not typically in driveways or parking lots. I ended with a question, thereby keeping control of the conversation. It was time for me to offer a tool anyway, so I made that my question.

Jack: Yeah, I would.

Comments: Of course, he would. The principles are irresistible.

Russ: By the way, my name is Russ (extending my hand to initiate a handshake), Russ McNeil.

See: What's Your Name, Jack?
Comments: Up to this point, we still didn't know each other's names. It was time to rectify that situation.

Jack: My name is Jack.

See: What's Your Name, Jack?
Comments: You knew his name was Jack, didn't you?

Russ: Hang on Jack and I'll get you something to look at. (I reached into my car and grabbed a magazine.)

Principle: Casualize & Minimize.
Comments: Have a magazine and / or a DVD inside your car where you have easy access. You don't want a prospect to see a whole stack of them. The process should appear to Jack as spontaneous and unpracticed.
Notice the casual speech ("Look" instead of watch or read and "something" instead of DVD or magazine). There's nothing wrong with the other terms. They certainly are not red flag phrases. It was simply a matter of my automatic pilot choosing alternatives on the fly. This an example of unconscious competence as discussed in Chapter 2.
(I handed the magazine to Jack. He took it and glanced at the cover)

Jack: What's this about?

Comments: I assume he's asking about the magazine (The Most Dreaded Question).

Russ: It's about taking advantage of some unique timing in the market place. This is real simple, Jack. If you like what you see, we get together for half a cup of coffee and fill in the gaps. If not, we're done and I won't even need the magazine back. Make sense?

Principles: Casualize & Minimize, Feeding the Birds, Who Let the Dogs Out? Comments: This one phrase emphasized simplicity, introduced doubt, and gave him permission to decline. There was virtually no chance of him saying "no."

Jack: Yeah.

Comments: You can see how the conversation was building momentum. It was getting easier an easier for Jack to answer yes to my questions.

Russ: Okay. All I ask in return is a daytime number so I can see if there's any common interest. Is that fair?

Principle: Feeding the Birds
See: I've Got Your Number Now
Comments: Of course, it's fair and Jack knew it. Furthermore, he was about to admit it . . .

Jack: That's fair.

Comments: He bought in to giving his number.

Russ: Great. (As I pull out my phone) What's the best number to reach you at? (I enter the number in my phone and show it to him.) Did I enter it correctly?

See: I've Got Your Number Now
Comments: Notice how I ended with a question. Even a question as simple as this one leaves you in control.

Jack: That's it.

Comments: The conversation was about over. It was time for me to set his expectations.

Russ: Okay, Jack. This is a crazy week for me. I'm not sure exactly when I'll be calling but, you have my word that I'll give you a buzz sometime over the next two or three days. Sound good?

Principle: Mental Judo, Casualize and Minimize
See: Follow Up or Fall Down
Comments: This set Jack's expectation of my call. It also told him that I'm busy just like him. Not only did this introduce Mental Judo it also

addressed the time objection by telling Jack that busy people can do what he saw me doing. Notice the use of the casual term "buzz."

Jack: Yeah.

Russ: I'm glad we bumped into each other (as I offer to shake his hand again).

Comments: Notice that I did not say "I'm glad I bumped into you." I said "we." This made Jack partly responsible for the conversation, which in turn, portrayed more spontaneity. The second handshake wasn't required. It can create the feeling of "cinching the deal," but I typically avoid doing it with overly cautious prospects (Greens and, sometimes, Yellows).

Jack: Me too.

Russ: Have a great day.

Comments: I prefer to get the last word in by ending on a positive note.

The End

So, Russ, What Happened Next?

The curious reader may be wondering how this particular prospecting effort turned out. Well, he chose not to join my team, but he did become a customer. And, the next time I meet someone in advertising, I have an indirect connection to draw upon. All in all, I'd say it was worth stopping for gas.

You've Come a Long Way, Baby

Congratulations! You have weaved and bobbed your way through 18 chapters of principles, laws, tips, and scripts. Everything you need to know about becoming a master prospector is contained within these chapters. Only two things remain — committing to personal development and practicing. To know and not do, is not to know. The ball's in your court.

Now...go knock 'em *alive!*

About the Author

Russ McNeil didn't exactly enter the world of team building having the skills necessary to be an instant success. With an overbearing personality, a disinterested warm market, and a genuine fear of approaching strangers, he had significant obstacles to overcome. And overcome them he did. Through trial, error, diligence, and determination, he eventually mastered the art of prospecting strangers.

For several years, Russ prospected and sponsored strangers using what he had learned from personal experience. He had no idea that his prospecting skills were so finely honed. One day, his mentor and up-line "big pin", observed Russ prospecting in a restaurant. He immediately asked Russ to begin training other reps. Before long, Russ was training at both private and corporate sponsored sessions.

Russ soon realized that there is a hunger for pure, hard-hitting information on situational prospecting. While feedback from the live trainings was overwhelmingly positive, his seminars were limited. Time constraints simply did not allow for complete end-to-end explanations of the in's and out's of prospecting strangers. To the author, the need for a book on the subject was obvious. Three years later, *Prospecting Rules! (the unbranded version of Prospecting Power!)* was born. And that's how Russ McNeil became known as the "Guru of the 6-foot rule."

Russ resides in north Texas with his wife of 25-plus years, their three sons, and Milo, a beagle who excels at prospecting rabbits.

Russ is surprisingly accessible through his website, AhaUniversity.com, or AhaUniversity@gmail.com. Feel free to drop a note to introduce yourself or to comment on his work.

If you find the information in this book useful, you may also enjoy the author's complimentary newsletter, *Prospecting with Purpose.* It's loaded with even more great information about prospecting like overcoming fears, mindset, prospecting affirmations, and more. (Note to team leaders: the newsletter is informational in nature. It does not promote any business opportunities.) Visit AhaUniversity.com to subscribe.